Classroom Diversity

Classroom Diversity

CONNECTING CURRICULUM
TO STUDENTS' LIVES

Edited by
Ellen McIntyre
Ann Rosebery
Norma González

HEINEMANN
Portsmouth, NH

Heinemann
A division of Reed Elsevier Inc.
361 Hanover Street
Portsmouth, NH 03801–3912
www.heinemann.com

Offices and agents throughout the world

Library of Congress Cataloging-in-Publication Data
Classroom diversity : connecting curriculum to students' lives / edited by Ellen McIntyre, Ann Rosebery, Norma González.
     p.   cm.
     Includes bibliographical references and index.
     ISBN 0-325-00332-7
     1. Multicultural education—United States—Curricula—Case studies.   2. Socially handicapped children—Education—United States—Curricula—Case studies.   3. Learning—Social aspects—United States—Case studies.   I. McIntyre, Ellen.   II. Rosebery, Ann S.   III. González, Norma.
LC1099.3 .C52 2001
370.117—dc21

                                                                                            00-061388

Editor: Leigh Peake
Production: Elizabeth Valway
Cover design: Joni Doherty
Manufacturing: Louise Richardson

Printed in the United States of America on acid-free paper
05   04   03   02   01   DA   2   3   4   5

Contents

Acknowledgments

We thank the children and their families about whom these stories are written. We thank the teachers, administrators, and researchers who have worked diligently with the children and their families on connecting school curricula to students' lives. Their deep commitment to creating excellent educational programs for students of diverse populations is inspirational. We thank the Center for Research on Education, Diversity, and Excellence (CREDE), one of the national centers of the Office of Educational Research and Improvement at the U.S. Department of Education, for funding the studies that have produced the stories in this volume. We thank Ruth Hilberg of the University of California–Santa Cruz for her support and assistance on this project. Finally, many thanks to Leigh Peake and Elizabeth Valway of Heinemann for their support of this project. Their belief in the importance of hearing the voices of students who have often been silenced in schools has kept us going. We truly hope this book makes a difference for teachers and students interested in educational excellence.

1

Connecting Students' Cultures to Instruction

ANN ROSEBERY, ELLEN MCINTYRE
& NORMA GONZÁLEZ

The population of children in the United States is rapidly becoming more ethnically and culturally diverse. At the same time, the population of white, middle-class, female teachers remains stable. This mismatch between children's home cultures and the cultures of schools plays havoc with student achievement. Disproportionately high numbers of minority, immigrant, isolated, and poor children perform consistently lower academically than white, middle-class students (Miller 1995). As Jonathan Kozol notes, "behind the good statistics of the richest districts lies the triumph of the few.

Behind the saddening statistics of the poorest cities lies the misery of the many"(1991, 158). This achievement gap has caused much consternation among educators, and how we address this growing problem will determine who gets properly educated in the twenty-first century.

What is behind the gap? Why do poor children fail more often in school? Why are students of color often left out of advanced academic work? As educators and researchers, we hear these questions on a regular basis. Like others, we have no quick or easy answers. Indeed, we feel there is no *single* answer. Complex issues require complex answers, and there is no silver bullet that can reduce poverty, differential access, and educational disparity to manageable sound bites.

We believe, however, that some of the educational research done in the last twenty-five years has much to say about the design of classrooms in which today's minority and working-class children can be successful. The work we are referring to, sometimes called a sociocultural approach, tries to understand learning as the result of social interactions among the individual, society, and culture (Rogoff 1990; Tharp & Gallimore 1993). This approach suggests that minority and working-class children can succeed in school if classrooms are reorganized to give them the same advantage that middle-class children always seemed to have had: instruction that puts their knowledge and experiences at the heart of their learning.

Understanding Sociocultural Research

To explain our point of view, we begin by sketching a brief history of the relevant research for our readers. Beginning in the 1960s, researchers from disciplines such as anthropology, cognitive psychology, education, sociolinguistics, and sociology started asking questions about the educational disparities that exist among middle-class, suburban (and principally but not exclusively white) children and working-class and poor (and principally but not exclusively minority) children. These researchers wanted to know why our schools were failing these children. Not surprisingly, no single answer emerged. However, if one looks across these studies, a pattern emerges that we believe speaks directly to teachers and schools.

This research shows that children from different home, community, and economic backgrounds learn different "funds of knowledge," to use the words of Carlos Vélez-Ibáñez and James Greenberg (1992), and that these funds of knowledge are not treated equally in school. We are using the phrase *funds of knowledge* broadly, to mean the various social and linguistic practices and the historically accumulated bodies of knowledge that are essential to students' homes and communities (González 1995a; Moll et al. 1992; Vélez-Ibáñez & Greenberg 1992).

In her influential study *Ways with Words,* Shirley Brice Heath (1983) described the language practices of three communities in the rural Piedmont Carolinas. One was a working-class, predominantly white community, one was a working-class, predominantly black community, and one was a middle-class community with a history of formal schooling. Working in cooperation with teachers and local residents, Heath found that although the people in these communities lived within a few miles of one another, they socialized their children into talking, reading, and writing in profoundly different ways.

As she followed the children into school, she found that their different language practices carried implications for their academic success. The children from the working-class families, both black and white, fell behind in school—some early on, others more gradually—and eventually dropped out. Children from the middle-class families, while not all top scholars, graduated from high school.

It is important to point out that Heath found that the children of all communities were immersed in rich and stimulating language environments. Early on, they all learned to value stories and printed texts; they were encouraged to listen to, practice, and try out the various forms of talk used in their communities; and they were all impressed with the importance of doing well in school.

Building on Heath's work, other researchers described the discontinuities that children from diverse backgrounds can experience between the worlds they know at home and the world of school. To varying degrees, these children may find that they do not know how to show the teacher what they know in ways she can recognize. They may be asked to engage in activities they do not fully understand. And they may find that the teacher talks in ways that are unfamiliar and confusing. From the start, minority and working-class children can find school a confusing and sometimes uncomfortable place (Ballenger 1999; Delpit 1995; Gallas 1994; Gee 1990; Heath 1983; Michaels 1985; Paley 1979; Philips 1972; Purcell-Gates 1995; Tharp & Gallimore 1993).

Children from middle-class homes, where the funds of knowledge correspond nicely to those of school, experience much less discontinuity. For example, they know what the teacher is talking about most of the time and if they don't, they know how to ask for help in ways the teacher recognizes. They are likely to know how to tell stories in ways the teacher understands. They can talk about objects and experiences in decontextualized ways, that is, outside the situation in which they were experienced, and they have learned how to organize and remember objects according to abstract attributes, for example, physical characteristics, functions, or spatial characteristics (Heath 1983; Michaels 1985; Wertsch 1985).

It seems that middle-class children and children from families with a history of formal schooling learn these funds of knowledge at home because they need them to be functional, contributing members of their families and communities. It also happens that these funds of knowledge are closely aligned with those valued at school. Because of this, middle-class children enter preschool and kindergarten already knowing much of the stuff of school. Right from the start, they know what to do and what to say in order to have their ideas heard and their activities valued by the teacher and the school.

Minority and working-class children likewise acquire funds of knowledge at home. Not surprisingly, they learn those things that enable them to be useful and productive members of their families and communities. In recent years, researchers and teachers have begun to describe the rich and varied funds of knowledge these children learn at home. They include specialized knowledge of mathematics, science, and history; knowledge of how to tell stories from memory that require the orchestration of a number of different people, places, and events; command of a range of creative, poetic, and dramatic uses for language; and familiarity in making imaginative connections with natural phenomena. Unlike the funds of knowledge that middle-class children learn at home, however, these funds of knowledge often go unrecognized in school. And in some cases, they may actually be in conflict with those valued in school (Ballenger 1999; Gee 1990; González 1995a; McIntyre et al. 1999; Michaels 1985; Tharp & Gallimore 1993; Vélez-Ibáñez & Greenberg 1992; Warren & Rosebery 1996).

During the late 1970s and the early 1980s, Western psychologists and educators learned of the work of the Soviet psychologist Lev Vygotsky (1978). Vygotsky spent much of his career studying how children learn and describing learning as a process that involves social as well as cognitive transformations. His writings emphasize how interactions between people are central to the ways in which individual learning and development occur. He argued that children internalize the kind of help they receive from others and eventually come to use it independently to direct their own problem solving.

For Vygotsky, the shift from needing help to accomplish a task to accomplishing it independently constitutes learning. Central to his theory is the belief that children learn best when parents and teachers create instructional activities that use what children already know as resources for learning new knowledge and practices.

Building on this research, educators began to see teaching and learning in a new way. They realized that, from this point of view, the curricula in most

American schools seem to build almost exclusively on the funds of knowledge of middle-class children. Some wondered what would happen if the curricula in schools that served minority and working-class children were revised to leverage their funds of knowledge as resources for learning. With this in mind, a new line of classroom-based research emerged.

Putting Students' Funds of Knowledge First

The teachers and researchers who were asking these questions realized quickly that they were breaking new ground. In some cases, they found that they did not know enough about students' funds of knowledge to move forward. In other cases, they found that they had to challenge basic and pervasive assumptions about what and how minority and working-class children learn in order to accomplish their goals.

Some began by examining how minority and working-class children spend their time in the classroom. Research in urban classrooms showed that reading instruction for most working-class and minority students, for example, focuses on learning decontextualized skills and subskills rather than on making meaning (Anyon 1980; Goodlad 1984; Moll et al. 1980; Oakes 1986). Students spend their time practicing skills associated with phonics, spelling, and grammar in isolation from their home-based oral and written literacy skills. They complete workbook pages and drill sheets instead of using and expanding their knowledge of these skills while engaged in meaningful reading and writing activities. In short, these researchers found that students' funds of knowledge are essentially absent from reading instruction in urban schools.

Lest we be misinterpreted, we think it is crucial for all students in American classrooms to become fluent readers, writers, spellers, and speakers of Standard English. What is open to question for us, however, is *how* students learn these things. We believe that a false and unexamined assumption underlies a heavily skills-oriented approach to reading: that minority and working-class students need to master the "basics" before they can—or should—engage in "higher order" literacy activities. From our point of view, this assumption ignores the fact that all students, regardless of background, use oral language on a daily basis to engage in sophisticated acts of literacy and communication, including argumentation, interpretation, and critique, in the schoolyard, in the hallway, at home, and elsewhere.

If a sociocultural perspective finds an exclusively skills-based approach to reading problematic, what kind of instruction would it suggest? One of the most comprehensive efforts to implement a sociocultural approach to learning and teaching took place at the Kamehameha Early Education Program

(KEEP). KEEP represents a broad-based, interdisciplinary effort to improve the education of children of Polynesian descent, Hawaii's indigenous minority. To improve students' reading ability, instruction was redesigned from a phonics-based program to "direct instruction of comprehension" through the discussion of stories. After the new program was put into place, KEEP staff noticed that in some classrooms, the discussions gradually took on an overlapping-turn structure similar to the overlapping speech common in ordinary Polynesian conversations and in a public storytelling event called "talk-story."

In talk-story, a story is co-narrated by at least two people and the speech of the narrators is overlapped by audience response. It is practiced widely throughout the Polynesian community in Hawaii and, as such, is part of the children's home-based funds of knowledge. The KEEP teachers and researchers found that when a teacher was willing to relax her control of turn taking, the children gradually introduced the talk-story form into the new reading comprehension discussion format. Some teachers, aware of the changes introduced by the children, began to experiment with the discussion format. Instead of addressing questions to specific individuals, for example, a teacher might address her questions to the group. Teachers found that children volunteered answers with unexpected enthusiasm, often chiming in and overlapping one another's turns.

Teachers and researchers paid close attention to this emerging instructional interaction and its effects on students' participation and learning. They noticed that when teachers allowed what they eventually called "instructional conversation" to go on, the children participated more, had a higher number of correct responses to teachers' questions, and offered a greater number of ideas and logical inferences related to the story's content than they did during more traditional question-answer sequences. In other words, the students learned more and performed better when they were allowed to use household-based funds of knowledge, in this case particular features of the talk-story form, to support the development of reading comprehension (Au 1980; Jordan 1985; Tharp & Gallimore 1993; Tharp et al. 1984; for a discussion of the KEEP reading program, see Cazden 1988).

Enlarging Sociocultural Approaches

By emphasizing the social and cultural situatedness of learning, sociocultural approaches served as a counterpoint to models of learning as structured individualized cognition. They helped conceptualize the notion of *difference* rather than *deficit* in learning. In the years since these initial studies were carried out, however, shifting theoretical landscapes have begun to problematize aspects of sociocultural theory and the sometimes unanticipated ways it has been taken up and interpreted.

For example, some research has assumed that culture can be embodied in particular learning styles and shared assumptions. This work assumed that all members of a particular group shared a bounded and integrated body of knowledge and that these norms shaped individual behavior. A basic tenet of sociocultural models is that children learn bodies of knowledge through guided participation in ongoing cultural activities as they observe and participate with others in culturally organized practices. In some instances, these points of view led researchers to characterize communities of diverse students according to sets of "shared" traits. Students from particular cultural, ethnic, or linguistic backgrounds were stereotyped as "nonverbal," "field-dependent," or "kinesthetically oriented."

However, as researchers and educators looked more closely at diverse communities and their activities, they realized that these communities, like all communities, are constantly in transition, that the meanings and forms of activity that exist in any community are always being contested and negotiated by its members. From this point of view, previously assumed shared bodies of knowledge began to seem not so shared. It became clear that lists of characteristic traits could not accurately describe cultural, ethnic, or linguistic groups. Instead, researchers and educators found it more productive to attempt to describe the broader social, political, and economic conditions influencing students' lives in and out of school (Foley 1990; Willis [1977] 1981; see Levinson et al. 1996).

Enlarging sociocultural perspectives in these ways has helped us visualize the fluid and dynamic nature of students' experiences and the varied cultural practices in which they participate. And it has highlighted the shortcomings of approaches that attempt to characterize groups according to stereotypical traits. It shows that such lists are based on false assumptions about culture and its transmission and that no list can be flexible, dynamic, or complex enough to describe an individual's point of view, let alone the points of view of a group of individuals. Finally, it carries another important implication: because these characterizations fall short, it is a mistake to use them as the basis for instructional design and decision making. Instead, by focusing on practice—that is, on what households and communities actually do—we can bring the multiple dimensions of students' lived experiences to life in the classroom. One important result of such work is its description of the ways in which households and communities make use of their multiple cultural systems as strategic resources in their lives and work (González 1995b; Moll et al. 1992).

Practicing a Sociocultural Approach in the Classroom

In recent years, teachers and researchers have begun working together to explore ways of using minority and working-class students' funds of knowledge as the centerpiece of instruction. But doing this is easier said than done. It provokes a host of questions. How can teachers know what funds of knowledge their students bring with them into the classroom? How can they know which of the many rich and varied funds might become a productive foundation for teaching school-based funds of knowledge? The stories in this book attempt to answer such questions through rich descriptions of contextualized teaching, detailed by the Center for Research on Education, Diversity, and Excellence (CREDE).

This book illustrates how teachers around the country are engaging minority and working-class students in meaningful learning as indicated by some of the above practices. The stories show African American, Haitian American, Latino, Native American, and rural white students of Appalachian descent learning how to read and write and engaging with mathematical and scientific ideas and practices. All of the classrooms described here share one important characteristic: they use students' household-based funds of knowledge as resources for learning school-based funds of knowledge. Teachers and researchers sought to build on the deep connections between the classroom curriculum and the knowledge and practices of students and their households. They do not believe that a simple transmission of knowledge from the community to the school or from the school to the community will put the students' funds of knowledge first or result in authentic curriculum or pedagogical reform. Instead, each chapter tells how teachers and researchers sought to transform available knowledge bases for academic purposes and thus build bridges in nontraditional ways.

In Chapter Two, "Connecting Cultural Traditions," teacher Sharon Maher describes the challenge of acquiring knowledge of local norms from her students' homes and community in the Zuni Pueblo in New Mexico. Maher, in collaboration with Georgia Epaloose and Roland Tharp, explains how she designed activities for her middle school students that connected traditions from the Zuni culture and at the same time improved her students' expository writing skills.

In Chapter Three, "Ring My Bell," Michele Foster and Tryphenia Peele describe the many ways that teacher Vivette Blackwell uses her knowledge of her mostly African American students' community, cultural preferences, and linguistic abilities to create a classroom environment in which they are comfortable and expected to achieve at high levels. Vivette does this by providing opportunities for parents to participate in learning activities, planning her classroom activities around her students' knowledge and experiences, and helping them make connections between school, home, and community knowledge.

Chapter Four, "Unearthing the Mathematics of a Classroom Garden," by Leslie Kahn and Marta Civil, describes a teacher-researcher project in a fourth/fifth-grade classroom designed to better understand mathematics teaching and learning within an integrated unit. Leslie describes how she and her students developed an integrated curriculum, "From Weaving to Gardening," that filtered across disciplines from social studies to language arts to mathematics.

Chapter Five, "The Sound of Drums," by Faith Conant, Ann Rosebery, Beth Warren, and Josiane Hudicourt-Barnes, tells how a teacher of seventh- and eighth-grade Haitian students used everyday and scientific resources to develop an investigation into the science of sound in her classroom. Hudicourt-Barnes describes what she and her students learned as they jointly redesigned a science unit to take advantage of her students' knowledge of and experiences with drumming.

In Chapter Six, Maureen Callanan, Pilar Coto, Ligia Miranda, Anne Striffler, Jim Allen, Cherie Crandall, and Colleen Murphy describe how a group of teachers used what they call a "child-centered and contextualized curriculum" to engage preschoolers in science. They tell how their exploration of raising chicks in the classroom was jointly constructed by students and teachers and how, because the students' interests and questions moved the investigation forward, the unit unfolded in ways that could not have been anticipated by the teachers.

In Chapter Seven, "Agricultural Field Day," Ellen McIntyre, Ruth Ann Sweazy, and Stacy Greer describe how Ruth Ann and Stacy made visits to the homes of their students in rural Kentucky to better understand the children and the funds of knowledge they brought with them to school. As a result of these visits, Ruth Ann and Stacy designed a series of reading, writing, and mathematics lessons around a major annual school event: Agricultural Field Day. In this way, they used their students' extensive knowledge of farming and farming practices (e.g., seed types, growth rates of various plants, plant parts) as the basis for their ongoing curriculum.

In Chapter Eight, "Teaching History," by Ellen McIntyre and JoAnn Archie, we learn how JoAnn focuses on community building in her primary grade classroom and extends her instructional program from this philosophy. JoAnn, a native of the mostly African American community in rural Kentucky in which she teaches and resides, explains how she uses both her professional knowledge and her deeply personal understanding of her students, their families, and the community as the foundation of her teaching.

In Chapter Nine, "Creating Learning Communities," Melanie Ayers, José David Fonseca, Rosi Andrade, and Marta Civil tell how they discovered the mathematical funds of knowledge of Latino students in working-class neighborhoods and used them as tools for the classroom. José David, a seventh- and eighth-grade mathematics instructor, describes how he developed an architecture project called "Build Your Dream House" that engaged his students in a range of mathematical practices.

In Chapter Ten, "Creating Links Between Home and School Mathematics Practices," Norma González, Rosi Andrade, and Caroline Carson describe the methods used in their teacher study group to discover the mathematical funds of knowledge of Latino students in working-class neighborhoods and how this knowledge is used to enhance curriculum and instruction. This chapter provides a foundation for readers interested in learning how to begin understanding their students' and families' funds of knowledge.

Chapter Eleven, "Seeing, Believing, and Taking Action," by Norma González, Ellen McIntyre, and Ann Rosebery, sums up the ideas in this book by claiming that teachers who see, believe, and take action will be more likely to have students meet academic success in their classrooms. Specifically, teachers can (1) see every child as an individual with a wealth of cultural knowledge; (2) believe that their students can learn and that contextualizing instruction is one way of engaging their students; and (3) take action by getting to know the families and communities of the children they teach.

We hope these stories will be useful to those teachers who are searching for ways of going beyond the circumscribed area of the classroom and into communities. We hope the examples of what other teachers have done to re-design curricula and instruction around students' funds of knowledge will help you rethink your teaching. More than that, however, we hope that they provide a convincing rationale for "listening to what the children say," to use the words of Vivian Paley (1986), as a foundation for their learning and our teaching.

References

Anyon, J. 1980. "Social Class and the Hidden Curriculum of Work." *Journal of Education* 162 (1): 67–92.

Au, K. 1980. "Participation Structures in a Reading Lesson with Hawaiian Children: Analysis of a Culturally Appropriate Instructional Event." *Anthropology and Education Quarterly* 11: 91–115.

Ballenger, C. 1999. *Teaching Other People's Children: Literacy and Learning in a Bilingual Classroom.* New York: Teachers College Press.

Cazden, C. B. 1988. *Classroom Discourse: The Language of Teaching and Learning.* Portsmouth, NH: Heinemann.

Delpit, L. 1995. *Other People's Children: Cultural Conflict in the Classroom.* New York: New Press.

DiSchino, M. 1998. "Teaching Science from the Inside Out." In *Boats, Balloons, and Classroom Video: Science Teaching as Inquiry,* ed. A. S. Rosebery & 1B. Warren, 109–33. Portsmouth, NH: Heinemann.

Foley, D. 1990. *Learning Capitalist Culture: Deep in the Heart of Tejas.* Philadelphia: University of Pennsylvania Press.

Gallas, K. 1994. *The Languages of Learning.* New York: Teachers College Press.

———. 1995. *Talking Their Way into Science: Hearing Children's Questions and Theories, Responding with Curricula.* New York: Teachers College Press.

Gee, J. 1990. *Social Linguistics and Literacies: Ideology in Discourse.* Bristol, PA: Falmer Press.

González, N., L. Moll, M. Floyd Tenery, A. Rivera, P. Rendon, R. Gonzáles, & C. Amanti. 1995. "Funds of Knowledge for Teaching in Latino Households." *Urban Education* 29 (4): 443–71.

González, N., ed. 1995a. "Educational Innovation: Learning from Households." *Practicing Anthropology* 17 (3): 3–6.

———. 1995b. "Processural Approaches to Multicultural Education." *Journal of Applied Behavioral Science.* 31 (2): 234–44.

Goodlad, J. 1984. *A Place Called School.* New York: McGraw-Hill.

Griffin, S. 1992. *"I Need People" Storytelling in a Second-Grade Classroom.* Literacies Institute Technical Report Series. Newton, MA: Educational Development Center.

Hanlon, J. 1998. "Exploring Rust, Talking Science." In *Boats, Balloons, and Classroom Video: Science Teaching as Inquiry,* ed. A. S. Rosebery & B. Warren, 95–108. Portsmouth, NH: Heinemann.

Heath, S. B. 1983. *Ways with Words.* Cambridge: Cambridge University Press.

Jordan, C. 1985. "Translating Culture: From Ethnographic Information to Educational Program." *Anthropology and Education Quarterly* 16: 105–23.

Kozol, J. 1991. *Savage Inequalities.* New York: Crown.

Levinson, B., D. Foley, & D. Holland. 1996. *The Cultural Production of the Educated Person: Critical Ethnographies of Schooling and Local Practice.* Albany: State University of New York Press.

McIntyre, E., D. W. Kyle, R. Hovda, & N. Stone. 1999. "Nongraded Primary Programs: Reform for Kentucky's Children." *Journal of Education for Students Placed at Risk* 4: 47–64.

Michaels, S. 1985. "Hearing the Connections in Children's Oral and Written Discourse." *Journal of Education* 167: 36–56.

Miller, L. S. 1995. *An American Imperative: Accelerating Minority Educational Advancement.* New Haven: Yale University Press.

Moll, L. C. 1992. "Bilingual Classrooms and Community Analysis: Some Recent Trends." *Educational Researcher* 21 (2): 20–24.

Moll, L., C. Amanti, D. Neff, & N. González. 1992. "Funds of Knowledge for Teaching: Using a Qualitative Approach to Connect Homes and Classrooms." *Theory into Practice* 31 (2): 132–41.

Moll, L. C., E. Estrada, E. Díaz, & L. Lopes. 1980. "The Organization of Bilingual Lessons: Implications for Schooling." *The Quarterly Newsletter of the Laboratory of Comparative Human Cognition* 2 July (3): 53–58.

Moll, L. C., & N. González. 1997. "Teachers as Social Scientists: Learning About Culture from Household Research." In *Race, Ethnicity and Multiculturalism,* ed. P. M. Hall, 89–114. Vol. 1, Missouri Symposium on Research and Educational Policy. New York: Garland Publishing.

Oakes, J. 1986. "Tracking, Inequality, and the Rhetoric of School Reform: Why Schools Don't Change." *Journal of Education* 168: 61–80.

Paley, V. 1979. *White Teacher.* Cambridge, MA: Harvard University Press.

———. 1986. "On Listening to What the Children Say." *Harvard Educational Review* 56 (2): 122–31.

Philips, S. 1972. "Participant Structures and Communicative Competence: Warm Springs Children in Community and Classroom." In *Functions of Language in the Classroom,* ed. C. Cazden, D. Hymes, & V. John, 370–94. New York: Teachers College Press.

Phillips, A. 1993. "Raising the Teacher's Voice: The Ironic Role of Silence." In *Children's Voices, Teacher's Stories,* ed. Brookline Teacher Researcher Seminar. Technical Report No. 11. Newton, MA: The Literacies Institute, Educational Development Center.

Purcell-Gates, V. 1995. *Other People's Words: The Cycle of Low Literacy.* Cambridge, MA: Harvard University Press.

Rogoff, B. 1990. *Apprenticeship in Thinking.* New York: Oxford University Press.

Rosebery, A. 1998. "Investigating a Teacher's Questions Through Video." In *Boats, Balloons, and Classroom Video: Science Teaching as Inquiry,* ed. A. S. Rosebery & B. Warren, 73–80. Portsmouth, NH: Heinemann.

Rosebery, A., B. Warren, & F. Conant. 1992. "Appropriating Science Discourse: Findings from Language Minority Classrooms." *Journal of the Learning Sciences* 2 (1): 61–94.

Sylvan, L. 1996. "Getting Started with Science Talks." In *Teachers' Perspectives on Children's Talk in Science.* TERC Working Paper No. 2–96: 31–46.

Tharp, R., & R. Gallimore. 1993. *Rousing Minds to Life: Teaching, Learning and Schooling in Social Context.* New York: Cambridge University Press.

Tharp, R., K. Jordan, G. Speidel, K. Au, T. Klein, R. Calkins, K. Sloat, & R. Gallimore. 1984. "Product and Process in Applied Developmental Research: Education and the Children of a Minority." In *Advances in Developmental Psychology,* ed. M. E. Lamb, A. L. Brown, & B. Rogoff, 91–144. Hillsdale, NJ: Lawrence Erlbaum Associates.

Vélez-Ibáñez, C., & J. Greenberg. 1992. "Formation and Transformation of Funds of Knowledge Among U.S. Mexican Households." *Anthropology and Education Quarterly* 23 (4): 313–35.

Vygotsky, L. S. 1978. *Mind in Society: The Development of Higher Psychological Processes.* Cambridge, MA: Harvard University Press.

Warren, B., & A. Rosebery. 1996. "'This Question Is Just Too, Too Easy!': Students' Perspectives on Accountability in Science." In *Innovations in Learning: New Environments for Education,* ed. L. Schauble & R. Glaser, 97–125. Mahwah, NJ: Erlbaum.

Wertsch, J. 1985. *Vygotsky and the Social Formation of Mind.* Cambridge, MA: Harvard University Press.

Willis, P. [1977] 1981. *Learning to Labor: How Working Class Kids Get Working Class Jobs.* New York: Columbia University Press.

2
Connecting Cultural Traditions
Making Comparisons

SHARON MAHER, GEORGIA EPALOOSE
& ROLAND THARP

Nestled among the red mesas of the western New Mexico desert is a small living community that is also one of the ancient pueblos of New Mexico. Of the 10,000-plus population, there are approximately 2,100 school-age children who attend two public elementary schools, a middle school, two high schools, and two religious schools. Geographically isolated, the community retains a distinctive flavor through its history, language, and culture. The people are renowned for their fine inlay and overlay jewelry work; many are artists with international reputations; many continue the traditions of farming, hunting, and herding; many men and women are employed by agencies or businesses in the pueblo or in Gallup, thirty-five miles away; too many are unemployed. The ancient religion is alive, ceremonially rich, and basically unchanged since Coronado discovered the community in the sixteenth century. This is the pueblo of Zuni.

Here, late on a Friday afternoon after the last middle school bell has rung and all students have headed home, Sharon stares at the computer. She is ready to plan the next instructional unit for her eighth graders. Sharon has taught eighth-grade language arts for three years at Zuni Middle School (ZMS), but she is not from this community and does not speak Zuni, the first language of her students. How can she begin to plan her lesson?

Planning a Contextualized Unit

At the top of the computer screen, Sharon has entered an excerpt from her professional development journal. As she reads over the entry, she reflects, "This is what I believe":

> As an educator, I must bring to the classroom everything I know about how children learn and especially how Zuni children may learn. Sometimes "how they learn" means I must think quite differently about teaching a Zuni child. Connecting learning to students' personal, family, and community experiences is essential to my effectiveness as a teacher. The bonus is learning about a culture and language that is different from my own.

Sharon reviews and outlines her goals. In this unit, she plans to focus on writing skills. Students are to concentrate on three different types of writing in preparation for an upcoming state-mandated writing assessment. The instructional goal for this second-quarter grading period is for students to learn how to compare and contrast. She has chosen a nine-week theme of traditions—in the home, school, and community—focusing on expectations, rules, and responsibilities of community members. She decides to compare and contrast two diverse traditions, two contrasting cultures. She wants a unit rich in opportunities to compare and contrast and to include the physical environment, the seasons, and the multitudinous activities at school and in the community.

As Sharon begins the outline, she thinks about all the skills needed to integrate such a unit. She has been working this year with Georgia, her Zuni professional development consultant, and she is convinced that she can teach most effectively by relating new content to her students' prior knowledge and by contextualizing this unit in the knowledge, values, and experiences of her Zuni students. She decides to make Zuni itself one of the unit's two cultures.

"But do I know enough about Zuni to contextualize this unit?" Sharon wonders. Sharon's knowledge about this unique and somewhat mysterious community is not deep. She has been in Zuni for three years now, but there is a problem—a problem any teacher would face in a community very different from her own. It has been a challenge to acquire the knowledge base needed to contextualize most lessons. What knowledge resources are available to Sharon to help her understand her students' culture and daily life?

Acquiring Knowledge About Zuni Students

Sharon goes over the possibilities in her mind. What does she know about Zuni culture, and how did she learn it?

Through Reading

She has learned by reading historical and anthropological articles as well as cultural materials. Her researcher colleagues from the Center for Research on Education, Diversity, and Excellence (CREDE) have provided her with a wealth of information; she has read about Zuni diligently, and learned things such as the following:

> Zuni Pueblo is located on the Zuni Indian Reservation in the extreme west of New Mexico. The pueblo has occupied this site since 1692 and the tribe has occupied this territory along the Zuni River for at least a thousand years.... This country is remote, harsh and majestic....
>
> Historically, Zuni was a major contact point for trade long before the arrival of the Spanish conquistadors in the sixteenth century. During all the centuries of commercial, religious, and military invasions, Zunis have maintained their self-definition and traditional culture and religion. The Zuni language is predominant in homes and in all tribal government, religious, social, family, and cultural interactions.

In school, 96 percent of students are classified as limited English proficient (LEP). Instruction is in English, although the elementary schools employ bilingual classroom aides. The only use of Zuni language in middle or high school occurs when native teachers or paraprofessionals volunteer spontaneous classroom explanations and translations in Zuni. Zunis share with other Native Americans a history of schooling that ignored or attempted to destroy their culture and language by forbidding the use of Zuni language, Zuni religion, and Zuni cultural practices. In schools today there remains a residue of antagonism and alienation between school and home (Tharp et al. 1999).

Sharon knows that the problem of alienation is real and that it emanates from history and conflicting cultures, not from any lack of health, safety, comfort, or material resources at the school. In fact, the school is something of a physical oasis in the community. ZMS is a pleasant, thoroughly modern complex built in 1985 with plenty of space around the building for outside activities. The Zuni community is not a prosperous one, and 90 percent of the student population qualifies for federally funded free breakfast and lunch, which is provided through the school cafeteria. ZMS has a friendly social climate and an excellent teacher-to-student ratio. It offers four core curricula, two language arts teachers for each grade level, and electives such as physical/health education, art, computer lab, music, and band.

Despite this, the alienation between school and home persists; Sharon has no doubt about it. This year ZMS introduced a Personal and Social Responsibility class for students having difficulty adjusting to school. Approximately 35 percent of the student body is placed in this class for periods varying from nine weeks to the full school term, depending on the severity of classroom behavioral infractions. Sharon believes her book knowledge about Zuni history and society will help her understand the attitudes of the students, but it will not be enough to help her overcome students' alienation, their feeling that school is foreign, irrelevant, and unfriendly to them. To overcome that, she needs to bring her classroom alive for them, and that means she must know the experiences and concerns of her own students, this quarter, in her own classroom.

From Zuni Colleagues

Sharon turns her thoughts to her second resource, her Zuni colleagues. "Tyler," she thinks. In many ways, Sharon relies on the expertise of Tyler, the Zuni paraprofessional bilingual assistant for eighth grade. He assists her with lessons that are culturally sensitive. He often presents ideas to Sharon or the students about how to contextualize a particular concept, and as needed, he instructs students in their Zuni language. She has watched and listened to Tyler, and from him learned ways to connect what students know about their culture and community to the school content. Sharon has also seen how Tyler naturally and easily assists students in relating these contextualized concepts learned in the classroom back to issues in the Zuni community, outside of the school environment.

"And," Sharon thinks, "Georgia is an excellent resource." Herself a Zuni, Georgia was a parent of a ZMS student long before she was a teacher there; she has personal, cultural, and professional knowledge that Sharon draws on often, in long conversations about how to make her classroom more effective.

"Even so," Sharon reflects, "I need my own knowledge, I need to listen and observe and question and share with Zuni people if I am ever to really know the lives of my students." That, however, is not as easy as it once seemed.

By Living in the Zuni Community

Because very little rental housing for noncommunity people is available, Sharon and her husband, also a teacher, live in what is called a teacher compound, or complex, referred to locally as a "teacherage." All three teacherages are within walking distance of each school. These segregated complexes make it difficult for teachers to participate in the community and to interact with Zuni people in a social environment or in community activities. Furthermore, because of the nature of the complex Zuni religious system, many community activities do not allow participation, or even observation, by non-Zunis. Although Sharon's life in Zuni is comfortable, her isolation and de facto segregation limit her opportunities to develop a deeper understanding and knowledge of local norms. This is a serious problem for new teachers coming into Zuni, and many never overcome it.

From Students

"Of course!" Sharon thinks, and smiles. "The students can teach me about Zuni, while I'm teaching them about culture." The idea that she has twenty Zuni culture members in every class session pleases Sharon, and her mind races forward. Students will be her major resource for contextualizing the unit in their own culture. But how can she get them to participate actively and enthusiastically? Sharon knows the answer to that one: it is through dialogue, through listening and talking, that she can get them involved.

Sharon recognizes that dialogue is a critical tool for helping students construct new understanding in any subject. For Sharon, dialogue with her students will be equally important to building her own understanding. Hence, to most effectively help students learn about their Zuni culture, other cultures, and writing skills, she decides to practice instructional conversation (Tharp & Gallimore 1993).

Instructional conversation is a method for engaging students through dialogue, questioning, and the sharing of ideas and knowledge. Recently, Sharon heard a colleague mention the complexity and challenge of enacting this technique. Genuine dialogue between teachers and students on academic subjects is rare in many schools. Sharon is also aware of the difficulty Zuni adolescents experience with English oral expression. By eighth grade, they have become conditioned to listen to teachers' instructions and to respond in writing. Except for short-answer or recitation responses, they are rarely expected to respond verbally. Sharon knows that fostering student discussion, especially among students, would be an unfamiliar and probably uncomfortable task, both for herself and for her students. But she has no doubt that the gain is worth the risk.

So on this cold November afternoon, Sharon begins to put together all her thoughts for a unit of study that will ensure that by working together, she and her students will get the most out of the experience to come.

Formalizing the Plan

Synthesizing all her knowledge about effective teaching and learning, Sharon completes the final plan by designing a language arts instructional unit with a cultural focus. Sharon introduces the unit by communicating her expectations that she and her students will work cooperatively. She is very straightforward. "As an outsider to the Zuni community, I want you to teach me what I need to know about Zuni."

She then outlines the skills to be learned; the unit's goal; and the outcomes, projects, and types of assessments. By now Sharon's students are accustomed to her teaching style, her experimentation with teaching strategies, and her dedication to her own professional development, so they are not surprised when she tells them that they will all be learning a new strategy called instructional conversation. She is very open about both her own apprehension and her enthusiasm to learn and use this method. "You and I have to help each other," she tells her students. "I want you to be aware that there will be frequent videotaping of class activities, and other teachers will be in the classroom to assist with some of these activities. This is to help you evaluate your progress as students and to help me understand how I can make my lessons more meaningful for you. I will need your help and cooperation."

Some students are as apprehensive as their teacher. But Sharon also allows students to voice concerns before the unit is initiated. During this introductory period, Sharon makes connections with the previous unit of study and the continuing theme of traditions. One student is apparently worried that he will not be able to participate.

He asks, "What if your family is not traditional?"

"Have you lived in Zuni all your life?" Sharon asks.

"Yes, my whole life."

Sharon assures him that he knows a great deal about Zuni culture, both from observing his friends and neighbors and also from experiencing the more modern Zuni ways.

Introducing the First Culture: Zuni

The following day, to help students understand the meaning of *traditions,* Sharon begins with a whole-class brainstorming activity: defining *culture.* Together, she and her students construct a list of various elements of culture. Most students contribute to this list. Items they come up with include customs, as special practices that are common to one group; values, as beliefs of what is good and desirable; religion, as what is believed by a group and how it is practiced; clothing; housing; language; types of government; and traditional roles and responsibilities.

To introduce and guide the next task, the class creates a graphic organizer, the "Zuni Culture Chart" (Figure 2–1). Sharon wants students to provide concrete evidence or artifacts from the Zuni culture for the elements on the list they have just created during the whole-class brainstorming activity. Sharon reminds students that some elements are things that people do; such activities may not result in tangible artifacts, but students can list these examples and share them as well.

To introduce the next activity and prepare students for their future presentations in the unit, Sharon does frequent modeling and demonstrations to show students how to do what she expects them to do when making presentations. First, Tyler and Sharon model for students by presenting their own cultural items. Sharon shares a traditional Irish meal of liver and gravy over pancakes that her husband's family prepares for one of their traditional family gatherings. Tyler shows a display of bird feathers and explains the importance of feathers in Zuni culture, the types of birds used, and where to find and/or hunt them.

Beginning the next day, students brainstorm items used in cultural practice and start bringing in examples of these items: jewelry and clothing used during Zuni holidays and/or religious activities, such as blankets, sashes, pouches, and fetishes. Some students share photographs of family members dressed in traditional clothing and explain when, where, and why the photographs were taken. Over two class periods, students display such things as jewelry handed down by grandparents and a thimble used for sewing. For most students, this activity is an enjoyable task.

During this part of the unit, Sharon enlists the aid of a former student who recently won the title of Junior Miss Zuni at the pueblo's annual Zuni Fair. The Junior Miss pageant requires contestants to demonstrate a wide range of cultural knowledge and skills, such as traditional cooking, dancing, and pottery making. Junior Miss Zuni talks with Sharon's class about her experiences in preparing for the competition and how she gathered knowledge

Directions: Provide examples for each of the following elements of culture.

Holidays	Art/Music	Food/Drink	Clothing/Jewelry	Recreation
Shalako	Fetishes	Blue Corn Pudding	Sashes	Stick Races
Grandmother's Day	Fernando Cellicion (flute player)	Oven Bread	Turquoise Necklace	Fishing
Mudhead Payday	Pottery	Cedar Tea	Moccasins	Dances

Figure 2–1. *Zuni Culture Chart*

and learned from family and community members. From her presentation, students realize that cultural information can be used to accomplish a goal.

Introducing the Second Culture: The Jews of *Fiddler*

Once the students are involved with the task of linking elements of culture with concrete items, Sharon begins the unit's next phase. The first activity hooks their interest immediately; they watch an introductory section of the film *Fiddler on the Roof.* This movie depicts elements of Jewish culture at a particular time and place, and although Sharon realizes this fictional work is not an ethnography, she thinks it presents customs in a dramatic and fascinating way.

After viewing only a ten-minute clip, the students are already buzzing about the similarities and differences between the *Fiddler* and Zuni cultures. Sharon has them review the class-generated list of cultural elements and write down some examples of the traditional roles and responsibilities for each family member in the movie's Jewish community. They view the rest of the movie with an understanding that students are to watch for specific evidence and/or items to use in the creation of a graphic organizer showing the class-generated list of cultural features/elements with specific examples from the *Fiddler* culture.

Students then focus their attention on one specific feature of culture, such as traditional roles and responsibilities of family members. The class

Father	Mother	Son	Daughter
makes a living	takes care of children	chops wood	helps mother
religious head	cooks and cleans	goes to Hebrew school	takes care of garden
arranges marriages	teaches daughters	learns a trade	takes care of younger children

Figure 2–2. *Traditional Roles (from* Fiddler on the Roof*)*

constructs two lists: one detailing the traditional roles and responsibilities of Jewish family members and another describing the roles of Zuni family members (see "Traditional Roles," Figure 2–2). Once the two lists are formed, Sharon begins planning the instructional conversation activity.

Beginning the Instructional Conversations

At this time, Sharon assigns students randomly to groups so that she can teach through the dialogue of instructional conversation. For each of the groups, the goal is the same: to construct collaboratively, with teacher and students working together, a Venn diagram containing elements of Zuni and Jewish traditional family roles (see "Comparison of Zuni and Jewish Traditions," Figure 2–3). Starting this activity is not as daunting as Sharon had feared; she enjoys the conversations from the outset. But the students are not as comfortable with the dialogue process and are probably suspicious of this unusual teacher behavior. Sharon feels she talks too much at first and worries about it; she fills the silences because the students are not as vocal as she wants them to be. Georgia has warned her that although it seems like this kind of conversation should be easy and natural for eighth graders, it is not. Few classrooms provide students with the experience of extended teacher-student dialogue. And English language learners are especially reluctant to attempt complex communication in English. Initially, Sharon's students give her one-word responses or none at all, and Sharon begins to sweat.

But the development of an instructional conversation doesn't really take that long. Sharon's skillful questions and guiding comments draw the students into the conversation, and soon teacher and students are working together on topics of intrinsic interest to adolescents.

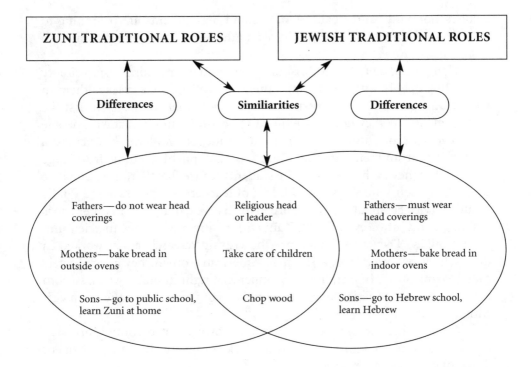

Task: Based on the movie *Fiddler on the Roof,* fill in the similarities and differences for each family member of the Jews and Zunis.

Figure 2–3. *Comparison of Zuni and Jewish Traditions*

"In the time and place of this movie, the Jews had arranged marriages. How would you feel about having a marriage arranged for you?" Sharon asks her students.

Everyone in the group has something to say about that. Not surprisingly, arranged marriage doesn't get much endorsement. Groans and "Noooooo"s predominate.

The students begin to connect what they know about their own culture to what they learn about Jewish culture as portrayed in the movie. Differences are identified quickly, but they soon begin to find similarities as well. Jeffrey says, "Zuni couples used to be matched up by their families." He adds that his grandmother had told him her own parents' marriage was arranged.

Sharon leads students to discuss how some practices in a culture change while others continue. Her students begin to see how cultures adapt to a changing world and how apparently different cultures can share common elements. Sharon is very pleased that through their use of instructional conversation and contextualization, she and her students are beginning to compare and contrast the Zuni culture and the Jewish culture as portrayed in *Fiddler on the Roof.*

Comparing cultures also assists eighth graders in taking responsibility for dealing openly with conflicting values and beliefs. Sharon leads them to see the advantages in diversity as well as the potential conflicts. At first the Zuni students say they don't have much opportunity to interact with people their own age from other cultures or with students who have experienced a life different from theirs; after all, Zuni is a small pueblo, remote from large cities. But as they exchange ideas, the students realize that there are nonnative students in their school, mostly children of teachers or doctors at the Public Health Service Hospital, and there are many native children from other tribes that come to visit or even live in Zuni with relatives who have married into Zuni families. They even remember the visiting researcher that worked in their school two years ago, a Japanese American woman they affectionately called Mama Sushi. In fact, they remember that right in their own classroom is a boy from Micronesia, attending school in Zuni while on a long-term visit with his relatives.

Considering the diversity even in their own isolated community, students are able to recognize the need to work cooperatively with students of different cultures and experiences.

At the end of the instructional conversation phase, Sharon reflects on the unit so far. She has been surprised to learn that many Zuni cultural practices are not basic knowledge for all Zuni students at this grade level. Thus, in using students' knowledge about their culture and comparing and contrasting Zuni with elements of Jewish culture as portrayed in *Fiddler on the Roof,* she has been able to provide her students with an extended opportunity for learning and reflecting on and synthesizing their thoughts about cultural issues in general and about Zuni culture, traditional and contemporary, in particular. The entire unit has given them an opportunity to initiate discussions with their parents and grandparents, asking about the uses and meanings of artifacts and the differences between today and the times of their ancestors. This phase of instructional conversation activities has actually run for two weeks longer than Sharon had originally planned! But she has no doubt it has been worth it.

Tackling the Writing Activities

After comparing and contrasting through instructional conversation, students are ready to tackle the next phase of the unit: reinforcing writing skills. Sharon's goals include teaching students to prepare an outline; to compose a paper comparing and contrasting two cultural groups; and to revise, proofread, and edit drafts. She knows, based on her experience teaching in Zuni, that she needs to present lessons on these topics clearly, either in small chunks or with step-by-step instructions. Throughout the writing process, she provides brief, small-group instruction with examples and models expectations to make sure the new material is connected to prior learning. For example, to assist students in composing introductory paragraphs with a thesis statement, Sharon develops a short writing task for each group: the creation of a thesis statement. The group's thesis statement then serves as an example for each member to use when writing the introduction for her or his individual paper.

Next, students develop outlines and then write their individual first drafts. Exercising the skills of editing and proofreading follows. Students do partner proofreading and editing of the first drafts, including going over structural skills such as grammar and spelling. Sharon reads and checks the final papers, evaluating them on content, complexity of understanding, and quality of comparison and contrast.

Many students make comments in the conclusions of their papers about how much they have learned from this activity. They now see themselves in light of another culture and begin to realize there are similarities between cultures. The most frequent type of statement communicated in the student papers is "No matter what your culture or your religion, you can always find something in common with a different culture."

Both Sharon's and the students' evaluations of the writing project are very positive. Most of the students rate it as "fun and interesting," a highly unusual response to a writing task. Sharon believes it went so well because the contextualization and instructional conversation activities prepared students for the writing activities. She writes in her own journal:

> In the process of engaging students in dialogue, through questioning and sharing of ideas and knowledge, students were able to write a paper that was meaningful and more helpful than the usual "compare and contrast."

Following Up

As a responsive educator, Sharon believes it is important to continue to apply and assess the use of newly learned skills. Therefore, even after the formal end of the instructional unit, she continues to design additional compare and contrast activities as contextualized opportunities arise. A favorite with students is comparing Halloween with the traditional Zuni Grandmother's Day, which is similar and occurs at about the same time of the year. These additional activities allow students to further use dialogue, jointly create products, and contextualize more frequently than usual throughout the entire quarter.

Reflecting on the Unit

Sharon and Georgia have reflected on this unit often, in conversation and in their own thoughts and writing. All the activities in this instructional unit were designed on the premise that developing language is a constructive, gradual, emerging process in which students grow in comprehension abilities and basic skills by processing texts in a generative manner, through building on their own experiences, knowledge, and values. By allowing students to bring their knowledge of their own culture to the foreground, Sharon helped them make meaningful connections to the compare and contrast process. Thus their comprehension of culture and their mastery of new thinking skills were greatly enhanced.

Georgia was particularly pleased that throughout all tasks, Sharon encouraged her students to learn more about themselves as Zuni people. Sharon encouraged them to discover the reasons for some of their traditions and to think about why some traditions have changed. This communicated to students that Sharon's interest in them was more than just a desire to develop their reading and writing skills.

Sharon knows that she grew professionally. She has become much more confident in developing the language skills of her Zuni students, through planning many and varied opportunities for students to spend time in dialogue with her and one another. She has a richer and more personal relationship with her students and is confident that she can produce that again, year after year. She is confident that she can assist students in perceiving multiple perspectives, and thus in becoming critical thinkers for their own individual success and for the success of the Zuni community. And she feels enriched by her own new knowledge of Zuni.

Here is the last entry in her professional development journal for this unit:

> Sharon, A− (showing improvement); Students, A+ (for teaching the teacher!).

References

Tharp, R., & R. Gallimore. 1993. *Rousing Minds to Life: Teaching, Learning, and Schooling in Social Context.* New York: Cambridge University Press.

Tharp, R. G., L. Hayes, R. Hilberg, C. Bird, G. Epaloose, S. Dalton, D. Youpa, H. Rivera, M. Riding-in-Feathers, & W. Eriacho Sr. 1999. "Seven More Mountains and a Map: Overcoming Obstacles to Reform in Native American Schools." *Journal for Education for Students Placed at Risk* 5: 5–25.

3
Ring My Bell
Contextualizing Home and School in an African American Community[1]

MICHELE L. FOSTER & TRYPHENIA B. PEELE

It's noon on a late January day in 1998. Most of Vivette Blackwell's[2] third-grade students are outside at recess; a few are sitting in the classroom eating lunch. At twelve thirty, students meander into the class. Three boys come into the classroom; the one in the middle, supported by one boy on either side, is limping. They tell Vivette that there was an accident on the playground. The limping boy announces, "I'm injured."

Addressing the expanding group of children who have come in from recess, Vivette smiles, her face brimming with excitement, and says, "He said *injured* and not *hurt*. Bring him over here and let him ring the bell." Smiling, but still limping, the boy rings the rusty bell sitting on the desk at the front of the classroom. Immediately after, the pupils sing one chorus of "Ring My Bell," a popular rhythm and blues song recorded by Anita Ward in the 1970s. In the excitement, the injured boy seems to have forgotten he was hurt.

Vivette introduced this ritual to her classroom in 1997 and invokes it to honor student learning. Ringing the bell while singing the words to the music is one way that this class celebrates accomplishment, which serves as an external confirmation that students are "soaring and flying," according to Vivette. Characterizing her classroom as a place where there's joy and humor along with seriousness and concentration, Vivette says, "We sweat; and we cry; and we fuss; and we fume; and we all have work to do; and we do not accept failure from *any* student. We sweat! We're all in there together."

This chapter examines how Vivette Blackwell provides opportunities for parents to participate in learning activities, plans her classroom activities around her students' knowledge and experiences, helps students make connections between school and home and community knowledge, and incorporates activities that draw on students' cultural preferences and build upon and extend students' indigenous linguistic abilities.

Background

Although she currently lives in a city across the bay, Vivette Blackwell, whose family migrated to California, grew up and attended elementary school in this now predominantly African American neighborhood and urban school district in Northern California. In 1997–98, her eighth year as a primary grade teacher at this school, she was teaching third grade.

Approximately three hundred students in grades K–5 attend Percy Julian Elementary School, located in a community perceived by many to be one of the most dangerous in the city. Fifty-three percent of the students who attend Julian Elementary receive free lunch while another 10 percent receive reduced lunch. A majority of the students at Julian—90 percent—are of color. Forty percent are African American, 15 percent Latino, 6 percent Chinese, 4 percent Filipino, 3 percent Native American, 0.07 percent Korean, and 22 percent come from other ethnic minority groups. Only 9 percent of the students attending Julian are white.

Although the overall percentage of students of color at Julian is comparable to districtwide percentages, because it is located in a predominantly African American neighborhood, the school has a larger percentage of African

American students than the districtwide figure of 17 percent. It also has a greater percentage of Native American students than the overall district figure of 0.07 percent and a smaller percentage of Latino and Chinese students than the overall district figures of 24 and 27 percent, respectively.[3] Because of its location in a predominantly African American neighborhood, Julian Elementary participates in the district desegregation order.

Julian Elementary sits halfway up a hillside, with some houses perched above it and others situated below. Built in 1974, the rose-brown concrete building is characteristic of schools of that period. The school's spatial organization also resembles schools built during the early seventies: several classrooms are arranged in two octagonal clusters at each end of the building.

Larger than some other classrooms, Vivette's room occupies one-quarter of a cluster. Inviting and visually appealing, the classroom is festooned with posters and signs. A sign at the classroom entrance advises, "Enter to Learn—Mary McLeod Bethune."[4] Another one high on the wall with orange-red letters shimmering against a black background proclaims, "Your mind is your most powerful resource." Signs with science words such as *physiology, botany, biology, entomologist, veterinarian, paleontologist;* suggestions for solving the mathematical problem of the day; strategies for approaching unfamiliar words; and dispositional states such as *perseverance* and *confidence* take up every inch of blank space. A life-size picture of an African American female police officer reads: "Children, it is illegal for second graders to read and skip over words they don't understand. Ask or look it up." A handwritten sign that says, "George Washington Carver Botanical Gardens Outside," hangs over the door leading out to the courtyard. Overhead a large sheet of newsprint written in hand-printed letters with the heading "Personality Words" lists about two dozen words such as *shy, selfish, mischievous, brave,* and *anxious.*

Students' creations adorn the walls and the ceiling. There is the usual student artwork, but there are unusual examples as well. One of the children's creations is a photograph of six students from this classroom, dressed in black with arms crossed, which proclaims, "Black Panthers Red Hot Readers Power to the Reader." The blackboard is filled with words and phrases—BOTANY IS THE STUDY OF PLANTS—Cam Jansen,[5] Science Projects—that hint at what the class has been studying over the past few weeks.

The class is organized into areas: a science observation area, where there are animals from each animal class (reptiles, amphibians, mollusks, arachnids, insects, and mammals), a reading and listening corner, and so on, as well as several configurations of desks. In the middle of the room is a large fiberglass pool with several pike swimming in it, surrounded by several varieties of large plants and flowers. There is a large open space in the front of the classroom close to the blackboard where children gather for large-group activities.

Twenty of the twenty-five students in this third-grade class are African American. Two of the remaining five children are of mixed-race backgrounds—African American and Korean and African American and Samoan. One pupil is white, one is Tonganese, and one is Latino. Sixteen of the students were second-grade students in this same classroom last year, and some of them were in this same classroom as first graders with Vivette. Each year she added a subsequent grade such that some of these children have been in her classroom for three years. This chapter includes two years of classroom observations conducted during the academic years of 1996–97 and 1997–98.

Talking About Thinking

To explicate her thought processes and model them for the children, Vivette frequently talks out loud as she goes about routine tasks. She believes that modeling the way she makes decisions is valuable for students because it teaches them to justify and be responsible for their own decisions. Once, before preparing to erase something on the chalkboard, Vivette reasoned aloud about what to erase and why. She said, "Let's see, I have a lot of things I don't want to erase." She scrutinized the chalkboard, assessing the value of each message. As she read each message, she circled it and commented on its importance. About the phrase NO FUN FRIDAY, she emphasized, "I don't want to erase that because you guys have to earn Fun Friday." Concerning the sentence reading BOTANY IS THE STUDY OF PLANTS, she commented, "I don't want to erase this because that's what we're studying." Settling on the name Cam Jansen, she explained, "I'm gonna erase 'Cam Jansen' (emphasizing the *en* sound) because now we know how to pronounce it." She concluded, "And I'm leaving up 'Science Projects' because that's what I'm going to talk about next." After this brief, reflective commentary, Vivette carefully drew a square around the empty space where the words Cam Jansen were once written, commenting, "I think I'll use this space."

Reading and Writing for Meaning

Vivette's students routinely participate in activities that are found in print-rich classrooms and that emphasize reading and writing for meaning (Bissex 1980). Specifically, students take part in paired and partner reading; they listen as their teacher reads chapter books aloud; they participate in writers' circle, where they compose stories, read them aloud to their peers (who ask questions), revise them, and read the final drafts to their classmates; and they take part in mini-lessons on topics ranging from how to make corrections on a writing assignment to story starters, descriptive language, and devices for grabbing the audience's attention. To illustrate, one day Vivette played a blues song for a while as students worked, then stopped the music and, using one particular stanza, drew students' attention to the lyrics by splicing them into a lesson on descriptive writing:

> The blues is when you really feel bad. Sometimes, you sing the blues because you really feel good, but this lady feels bad. . . . But do you hear that? She says there's nothing but a pain in your heart. Just like if you were writing a story about a character, you could say that the character had a pain in her heart. . . .

Most important, however, is that students use reading and writing to explore and connect with their personal and communities' cultures, histories, and experiences. They read, discuss, and write about current events and other matters pertinent to their national, state, local, and classroom communities. Sometimes they write letters to voice their opinions or take a position on issues that concern the class and especially those affecting their local community. Once when the city considered building a new mall in the neighborhood, the students wrote to the mayor advocating the conservation of trees and wildlife. They write thank-you letters to people who have visited their class, which often happens on Fun Friday, a Friday afternoon event in which students participate in one or more special activities typically related to something they learned in the classroom or encountered in a story. During one Fun Friday, a barber, the father of one of the students, talked about and demonstrated barbering. Earlier that week, students had read the book *Uncle Jed's Barbershop* (Mitchell 1998), and Vivette had sent home permission slips for students to receive complimentary haircuts. After the barber finished talking about his profession, students asked questions about the science of haircutting, and then several students received haircuts.

Talking Science

Vivette encourages students to observe and ask questions about everyday phenomena. Vocabulary development is a major focus in all subjects. Science is no exception. This was evident one day at toad feeding time. Vivette told a small group of students that they were going to observe which cricket the toad would eat first, the albino cricket or the ordinary cricket. She wrote the word *albino* on the board and asked the students if they knew what it means. When no one answered, she explained what the word means, offering a general definition of "having no color," and then passed around an albino cricket as she talked about how she came to acquire it. Through this activity students learned a new vocabulary word and how to observe carefully.

In addition to asking questions about the physical world around them, students compare metaphors expressed in proverbs or folk expressions to the actualities of the physical world. To illustrate, after children had misbehaved one day, Vivette asked, "How many of you have heard the saying, 'One rotten apple spoils the bunch?'" Several students waved their hands, and a chorus of voices exclaimed, "I have." She told the children that they were going to observe to find out whether the expression corresponds to the physical phenomenon. She passed a rotten apple around to students and asked if everyone agreed that the apple was rotten. Then she distributed several good apples and asked the students to verify that those apples were good. She asked several students to position the rotten apple in the center of a container and place all of the good apples around the rotten one so that all the good apples touched the rotten one. "Can one rotten apple spoil the bunch?" she asked. Each day for several weeks afterward, the students checked the apples, observing and writing down what they noticed.

As with her entire program of instruction, Vivette explicitly links science to the African American experience—personal and family lives, cultural backgrounds, political struggles, and historical and contemporaneous events. The class has learned about well-known and lesser-known black scientists throughout the centuries, including Percy Julian, the scientist for whom the school is named.

Another example: It's May and the Science Club is making plans for an outdoor garden to be named after George Washington Carver, an African American botanist whose life and career the students have examined during the year. Seated in a circle, the children watch as the teacher and four students, each holding a different garden tool, stand at the front of the classroom. Just as they are about to begin their conversation about the tools, a student asks a question about the homework, temporarily sidetracking the discussion.

Vivette: Did I say that? Let me see the homework. Hmm. Here is another whole-family assignment. Number one: Bring in a newspaper article. Number two: How many legs are in your home? How many human legs? How many animal legs? How many chair legs? How many bed legs? How many table legs? I should have had you count bug legs. Number three: How long does it take for an ice cube to melt? [To a student] Did you do that one? How long does it take an ice cube to freeze? Number four: Name five continents on the map or globe and find them. Memorize them for a prize. [To the teaching assistant] Phyllis, did you type that part in? Is that a mistype?

Phyllis: I typed that.

Vivette: Number five: What were your parents' favorite subjects in school and why? Some people are bringing back the homework with only the legs filled out. But I read that because I wanted to remind you you have to do all five of those things.

After reiterating the importance of completing and handing in all of the questions on the whole-family assignment, Vivette returns the students' attention to those holding the garden tools. For several minutes Vivette questions students about each tool, its name, how it is used in the garden and other settings. When one or more students offer an answer, pushing students to form their own opinions, Vivette characteristically probes, "How many agree? How many disagree?" This activity continues for several minutes, during which students talk about the tools and demonstrate several actions each performs in the garden as well as the result of this action on the terrain. Closing this instructional activity, Vivette announces that members of the Science Club will use these tools to transplant the seedlings into the George Washington Carver Botanical Garden but that before sowing the garden, the class will discuss each plant.

After lunch, the class meets again, this time to begin preparations for the students' science projects. After discussing various ways they can execute the projects, students break into two groups and go to separate areas. In one group, individual students are working on autobiographies that will accompany their science projects; in the other, individual students are formulating questions they would like to investigate for their projects. After half an hour, students switch tasks and continue working.

Later in the day, several students are seated around a table with Vivette. Each has previously chosen a word that describes a type of scientist to pronounce and spell for the class. One student raises her hand, spells *entomologist* and tells the class what an entomologist does. Another child tackles *physiologist.* A third, *botanist.* After several students have pronounced, spelled, and described their words, a student stumbles several times over the pronunciation of his word, *paleontologist.* "Suppose you borrowed money from your friend, Leon," begins Vivette, fashioning a story students can relate to, "and now you've got to pay him back. You've got to pay Leon. What have you got to do?"

"Pay Leon," the students answer in unison.

Using call and response, a highly interactive African American communicative discourse pattern, Vivette repeats the question several times and along with students answers the question, each time so that the intonation, rhythm, and stress clearly convey the phrase's meaning. Almost imperceptibly, she modulates the intonational pattern until it matches the first syllables of pale-ontologist (Piestrup 1973).

Connecting School, Community, and Family

The brief descriptions of classroom activities presented here illustrate several of the themes that organize the daily life in this classroom. Not only is this classroom a place where children are engaged, active, involved learners, it is one that integrates children's home, community, and school lives. Vivette provides numerous opportunities for parents to become involved inside or outside the classroom. For instance, parents can read stories, accompany the class on field trips, make classroom materials such as the list of personality words, lead a small group of children in an activity, or make a presentation to the entire class during Fun Friday, a period when children can choose among several novel but cognitively challenging classroom activities.

For those parents unable to participate in the classroom, there are many other ways to become involved in their children's learning. Whole-family assignments like the one described previously, which require parents' participation but do not require specialized skills on the part of parents, feature prominently in this classroom. Another way parents can participate is through Vivette's reading program. During the 1997–98 academic year, each of her students read at least one hundred and fifty books. Vivette enlisted parents to log the books their children read. If needed, she made calls to parents reminding them to hold their children accountable for reading and to hold themselves accountable for keeping track of the number of books read.

Having grown up and attended school here and taught in this community for a decade, Vivette is familiar with local community norms (Foster 1993, 1994; Ladson-Billings 1994). This familiarity enables her to design a variety of activities, many that draw on students' indigenous linguistic abilities and cultural preferences, including music, as illustrated in some of the examples here. Using familiar intonation patterns and varying them, Vivette helps students connect familiar linguistic patterns to other linguistic forms to help them learn difficult vocabulary words.

Students enjoy composing songs and performing them, often along with the latest dance steps. Rather than suppress these activities, Vivette incorporates them into her classroom. Students sometimes write songs with vocabulary words and then perform them. Both the teacher and students dramatize vocabulary words, an activity they use to highlight connotative meanings of words. The "Ring My Bell" ritual that opened this chapter is another example.

Throughout the day, students move among large-group, small-group, dyadic, and solitary activities. Music marks transitions, highlights particular moments, provides a soothing background, and occasionally serves as the basis for a lesson. Students' music preferences are honored, but they also listen to other genres. Students most often choose popular music; a favorite during 1997 was Selena's hit "I Could Fall in Love with You." But Vivette also plays classical music such as Luther Allison's *Clean Up Blues* or pieces by Mozart.

Even as Vivette honors community norms by embracing and incorporating students' cultural, musical, and linguistic preferences (Au & Kawakami 1994; Lee 1991; Piestrup 1973), she juxtaposes these with other forms and includes them in her reading, writing, and science instruction. This includes patterns of discourse that invite students and prod them to articulate a deeper understanding through talking aloud about the process of problem solving or decision making, practices that may not have been part of their habitual or preferred repertoire. The result is a classroom with increased motivation, fewer discipline problems, and higher student achievement.

As illustrated throughout this chapter, Vivette contextualizes teaching and learning in a variety of ways. She calls parents regularly, discovers their talents, and finds ways for them to come to the classroom to share them. Vivette also explicitly communicates to parents the role they play in her instructional program and is specific about what she wants them to do. Early in the year Vivette learns about her students' linguistic, musical, and cultural preferences, and finds ways to use these in her classroom. By getting to know her students and their parents, she is able to create a classroom in which children enjoy and take responsibility for their own learning. Making connections between home, community, and school knowledge, linking what students already know to the knowledge they need to learn, continually recycling new knowledge back to what students already know, and establishing a classroom community enable teacher and students to work through tears, celebrate joys, and rise to academic expectations together.

Notes

1. Acknowledgment: This work is supported under the Educational Research and Development Center Program (Coop. Agreement No. R306A60001-96), administered by the Office of Educational Research and Improvement (OERI), U.S. Department of Education. The findings and opinions expressed here do not necessarily reflect the position or policies of OERI.

2. Vivette Blackwell is the teacher's real name. All other names, including the schools, are pseudonyms.

3. The districtwide percentages for other ethnic minority groups are Japanese 0.09 percent, Korean 0.07 percent, and Filipino and other ethnic minority groups 11 percent. Only 11.5 percent of the district's students are white.

4. Mary McLeod Bethune, born in 1875, founded a school for black children in Daytona Beach, Florida, in 1904 that subsequently became Bethune-Cookman Institute, now Bethune-Cookman College. Later, McLeod Bethune took a position with the National Youth Administration under the Roosevelt administration. Active in civic affairs, she served as president of the National Association of Colored Women (NACW) and the National Council of Negro Women (NCNW).

5. Cam Jansen is a character in a popular children's book series.

References

Au, K. H., & A. J. Kawakami. 1994. "Cultural Congruence in Instruction." In *Teaching Diverse Populations: Formulating a Knowledge Base*, ed. E. R. Hollins, J. E. King, & W. Hayman, 5–23. Albany: State University of New York Press.

Bissex, G. 1980. *GNYS at Work: A Child Learns to Write and Read*. Cambridge, MA: Harvard University Press.

Foster, M. 1993. "Educating for Competence in Community and Culture: Exploring the Views of Exemplary African-American Teachers." *Urban Education* 27 (4): 370–94.

———. 1994. "Effective Black Teachers: A Literature Review." In *Teaching Diverse Populations: Formulating a Knowledge Base*, ed. E. R. Hollins, J. E. King, & W. Hayman, 225–41. Albany: State University of New York Press.

Ladson-Billings, G. 1994. *The Dreamkeepers: Successful Teachers of African American Children*. San Francisco: Jossey-Bass.

Lee, C. D. 1991. "Big Picture Talkers/Words Walking Without Masters: The Instructional Implications of Ethnic Voices for an Expanded Literacy." *Journal of Negro Education* 60: 291–304.

Mitchell, M. K. 1998. *Uncle Jed's Barbershop*. Old Tappan, NJ: Simon and Schuster.

Piestrup, A. M. 1973. *Black Dialect Interference and Accommodation of Reading Instruction in First Grade*. Berkeley, CA: Language-Behavior Research Laboratory.

4

Unearthing the Mathematics of a Classroom Garden

LESLIE H. KAHN & MARTA CIVIL[1]

Anyone walking into my (Leslie's) elementary school classroom during the recent school year would have been struck by a distinct absence of desks. They would have seen cubbies (cubicles) that housed everything from notebooks to pet rocks and tables that at times were overflowing with soil, pots, plants in various stages of growth, cardboard looms, pieces of yarn, and other artifacts of a busy classroom.

Our elementary school is small, with a population of fewer than four hundred students. It serves a multiethnic population. Hispanics are the largest minority represented at the school, constituting 35 percent of the student population. The desert is a natural part of the school site, which is situated in the foothills of the Tucson Mountains, with animals and desert plants a natural extension of our environment. Of the twenty-eight students in my fourth / fifth-grade class, most are bused in from a large area in the surrounding northwest region outside of the Tucson city limits.

Creating an environment that fosters collaboration while encouraging individual student-initiated inquiry demands constant reflection and anticipation of the students' needs. Over the years my teaching has changed to focus on blending the interests of the students with the curriculum. By structuring the classroom to connect to large themes, I have given the students more opportunities to delve deeply into subject areas, building their own connections to the curriculum.

A garden theme became a weaving/gardening thematic unit that incorporated social studies, language arts, and mathematics. The experience of developing such a unit reflects my beliefs and theories about how best to educate students. Throughout our weaving/gardening unit, problem solving motivated individual students to work together in teams; mathematics supported students' decisions as it became a common language in the classroom; and perhaps most important, authentic problems generated by the activities required solutions that were collaboratively planned and implemented. In what follows we share some of our experiences throughout the unit.

Brainstorming

At a summer retreat in the second year of BRIDGE (Linking Home and School: A Bridge to the Many Faces of Mathematics), a collaborative research project, participants listed mathematical connections we had seen in the homes of families that we had visited to determine the mathematical funds of knowledge our students possessed. While there were many other mathematical connections that could have been brought into the classroom, I chose to focus on gardening. The families that I had previously visited throughout the year had gardens; one grew vegetables, another grew flowers and more decorative plants. It seemed natural to choose gardening as the topic with the greatest potential for classroom connections. One other teacher in the group was particularly interested in developing a theme around gardening. The two of us, along with other project members, brainstormed ideas for a thematic unit that would be appropriate for students in grades 4 through 6 (see Figure 4–1).

In this brainstorming session I was both worried and excited at the same time. I was confident that the idea of having a garden would somehow fit into the district curriculum, but I wasn't sure how. When looking through the dis-

Garden Project

Storage of Plants
- harvest celebrations
- shelf life of organic food
- seeds/times to harvest

Resources
- home
- community
- costs/donations
- Who knows how?

Math Connections
- shadow and light
- drying plants
- proportion of seeds to plant
- water concerns
- planting spaces

Seed Art
- history of seeds
- origin of domestic seed
- shape study
- pod patterns

Native Plants
- cilantro
- squash
- Heritage Seeds
- nocturnals
- aloe vera
- cactus
- succulents

Literacy/Oral Language Development
- gardening stories
- children's literature
- family stories

EcoEnvironment
- medicinal/homeopathic
- biological/chemical pesticides
- companion planting
- fertilizers

bats (murcielago), hydroponics, grafting, growing season

Figure 4–1. *Web of Garden Brainstorm*

trict materials I found areas into which the project would fit: science, social studies, and mathematics.

During that daylong retreat I realized that I had been looking for an idea that would engage my students and me in mathematics and that was broad in scope. I wanted an idea or project that would encourage genuine mathematics inquiry, as well as being generative and collaborative.

Although I wasn't sure what the math would look like or how it would develop, I hoped that the amount of time it would take to make a successful garden would be realized in mathematics in the classroom as well. I wanted to be ready to support the students in a garden experience, address their interests, and have them provide real input as to how the project could work for the class. If the students were very disinterested or if I couldn't find an authentic way to work it into the curriculum, I would have lost interest and dropped the project. At that point in my thinking, the garden was an activity. However, it soon became obvious that it was a major part of the curriculum.

The curriculum set by the school district recommends a study of the Native Americans of Arizona in the intermediate grades. In response, our classroom focus for the year explored the tribal nation of the Navajos. We began the year by reading broadly from text sets about Native Americans. We watched videos portraying the tribe's involvement in herding and their uses of wool, as well as demonstrations of the wool being woven into blankets and rugs. The students' admiration of the weavings led us into discussions about how to create our own weavings.

Fascinated by the process of the sheared wool being spun into yarn, the students wanted to try to create the beautiful woven patterns they had seen previously. As a class, we decided to make our own weavings from yarn by first growing a garden to produce the colors for the dyes we would need, and so we began the weaving/gardening unit.

We asked the families to get involved at the annual Parent Open House. Their involvement was offered in many forms. Over time they donated books on Navajo weavings and rugs; they offered volunteer time in the garden; they spent time making and demonstrating how to use cardboard looms; they donated of seeds, soil, and flats of pansies and tomatoes; and they gave great amounts of encouragement. One family even volunteered their grandmother, an expert in preserving fabric artifacts, to talk to the class about weavings in Latin America. Although we eventually dyed only one yarn with the fruit of a local cactus (the prickly pear), the students' garden experience eventually impacted the curriculum in many more areas than creating weavings.

Seeding and Planting

Every morning we set aside time to work on some aspect of the garden unit. One of our first tasks involved a small group of students drafting a letter of explanation to describe the project to the families. One of the BRIDGE researchers, Marcia, helped the students design a survey to see what the families might be willing to donate to this project (e.g., by lending us tools, buying us some materials, or volunteering time in supervision or demonstration). Surveys went home and were returned within the week! We analyzed our surveys and were happy to note that almost all of the families supported our continuing requests for help. Six garden teams developed with four or five students in each team.

Fortunately for us, but not surprisingly, many of the students' families had gardens and the wisdom of many years of desert gardening. Digging in the ground would prove impossible, given the caliche (often sterile, rock-hard ground found in certain desert soils), and so we readily accepted donations of pots of any size. One family, whom I had made household visits to in the previous year, offered metal stakes and chicken wire to keep the javelinas (boars) out of our gardens. They had prior experience with javelinas coming into their own yard through an unlatched gate and destroying their vegetable garden. Javelinas are notorious for the massive overnight destruction of local gardens. Although some of the students initially wanted to make raised planters, in the end, we planted in gallon pots and whatever other containers the students brought from home and placed them in chicken wire enclosures.

We also invited the families for our first day of planting to help us build our enclosures and plant the first set of seeds. That day began on a clear morning in early October when the students, parents, two university researchers from the BRIDGE project (Marcia and Melanie), and I gathered outside of the classroom. Dressed in casual denim clothing, we were prepared to get dirty. One father, his work tool belt fastened around his waist, served as the expert on constructing enclosed areas. We carried the supplies—large pots, bags of soil, baskets of seeds, coils of chicken wire, and buckets for water—from the classroom to the designated area outside, near the classroom wall. By the end of the morning each group had built its own enclosure, complete with gallon pots filled with seeds.

Organization for this planting day in early October was the first of many experiences in which conflict arose. Students argued as to whether to plant vegetables or flowers; they resented having to work in groups that were not completely of their choosing; and they did not know if everyone would share the garden chores or if they could assign one person to each task. Because I had never tried to have a garden at school, the students quickly realized that I would not have the answers, but that I was an equal participant in this project.

The students and I dialogued about the problems involved in setting up a garden. Prior to the planting day, we set aside time twice a week for class meetings that gave the students a chance to voice their concerns about one another and negotiate the curriculum. Our questions frequently focused on interpersonal issues: How should we develop teams? Can friends work with friends? We also spent time discussing the more practical aspects of the garden: Would all vegetables grow? How much time could we have to garden each day? Finally we discussed how we were going to keep all of the information organized.

While it was difficult to find answers to the gardening questions (and assess which students could work with whom) without doing research outside of the classroom, we were able to find ways to organize what I consistently referred to as "our data." We decided on creating four sections in three-ring binders to organize the students' papers and become part of the experience.

The four sections were Notes, Drawings, Journals, and Experiments. The children were expected to routinely record their thoughts, observations, and measurements within the different sections of their binders. They did so with less resistance than they showed toward other classroom writing assignments.

The process of writing prompted the students to reflect on the experience (i.e., what they had just done, seen, or realized during the continuum of this activity) and see the plants with a more focused eye. Drawings formed an important aspect of our data collection process that the students used to envision what the plants would eventually look like. In the experiment section they recorded and graphed measurements of their own experimental vegetables as well as the class amaryllis we planted later in the year. Their notebooks also included their team calendar that each group devised to keep track of the watering schedule. As a class we agreed to overall scheduling structures so that the students knew how to care for their garden in general—Measurement Monday, Transplant and Thinning Tuesday, and Fertilizing Friday, for example. This became part of the larger system we devised for watering plants and completing assignments.

Uncovering the Mathematics

As we began the process of determining what mathematics the students could use to describe the garden, we first looked at how the class thought about mathematics in general. We had a whole-class discussion and invited Marcia and Melanie to participate and help with the process. We asked the class to explore the possibilities of a mathematics curriculum by uncovering the mathematics that the students noticed around them.

Trying to maintain order in the class was difficult; everyone had an opinion about mathematics. Marcia wrote the students' comments on butcher paper, I facilitated the conversation, and Melanie took observational notes. We wanted to hear the ideas and connections of all the students, not just the dominant few. The discussion following the question "How would you explain what mathematics is to a younger child?" was lively. Students offered a wide variety of responses, ranging from "helps count things" to "build things" to "symmetry, helps in everyday life" to "sets of big numbers." The students shared these and other ideas and then finished their thoughts in the journal section of their garden binders.

Writing became an integral part of our daily experiences with this unit. We also continually referred to this early discussion during our mathematics exploration, as well as when we were directly solving problems related to the garden, reminding the students of how many ways mathematics would help them in their garden.

The Tomatoes: Applying Business

One of the many mathematics talks that we engaged in happened because the plants kept growing and growing. The students did not believe that most of the seeds would germinate, and the pots were heavily overplanted. Jorge caused a major problem because he dumped an entire package of tomato seeds into his pot and kept it so well hidden that no one forced him to thin them. Soon we had eighty or more tomato plants and all of the enclosures were too small for the rapid explosion of plants.

Though the overplanting caused us problems, it was just what Jorge needed to become connected to school. He grew "his" tomato plants under grow lights within the classroom after their initial transplanting into cups. He was so proud of them and perhaps surprised at their survival that we were visited by both of his parents, a very rare occurrence at our school. After the plants outgrew their Styrofoam cups Jorge formed his own transplanting team and they repotted them into larger containers. We decided that we could set up a plant shop to sell the plants. He volunteered to write care sheets for them so that they would flourish in his absence. The development of the "How to Care for Your Tomatoes" flier was the first time that Jorge really needed to communicate in writing to the community at large. Because he was still transitioning from Spanish to English, this piece was difficult for him. But he was very motivated and that helped him succeed.

Jorge was not the only one who had resisted thinning. On Tuesdays and Thursdays the students were supposed to thin, but most of them just transplanted. Besides, as long as the plants kept producing tender, albeit small, vegetables, the students wanted to keep them. Our gardens soon became too small for the plants. What could we do?

The Chicken Wire Enclosures: Exploring Area and Perimeter

The challenge became determining how to have the most amount of space with the limited amount of chicken wire we had. This meaningful, real-life problem allowed us to discuss area and perimeter over several days. The talk focused on addressing the issue of perimeter and whether it affected the area of a shape and if so, to what extent. In the classroom we used color tiles, geoboards, and other hands-on experiences including drama activities to develop a deeper understanding of the relationship between area and perimeter. For example, the students worked together to create group charts and a class chart investigating the relationship between the perimeters and the areas of the shapes they made with tiles. They began to understand the relationship of a fixed perimeter, their chicken wire, to an ever-changing amount of space. In order to connect the informal mathematics of the garden with more formal academic mathematics, we introduced topics in measurement and geometry from the district curriculum.

We came back to the initial problem, namely, how to maximize the area given a fixed perimeter, through an in-class, hands-on activity. We gave each student a three-foot-long string, representing chicken wire, and asked him or her to make a shape that could represent the garden. They glued each shape to a piece of wax paper and then we followed up with a whole-class discussion centered around how we could find the area of an irregular shape (students were comfortable finding areas of rectangles). Some suggestions for finding the area included using their fingers, using their hands, and using objects to cover the shape. Some of these methods were actually linear rather than two-dimensional (e.g., using the length of one's fingers). But as the students shared and explained their ideas, they realized which methods would work and which would not. Then students set out to find the areas of their individual shapes. Most chose to use either tiles or cubes to cover their shapes. They then counted how many they used and found different ways to account for the gaps. Data for all the students were collected and this allowed for class discussion on which shapes seemed to have more area and which had less. Overall, students gave valid reasons for why they thought a circle would have a bigger area, mostly based on perception and counting.

The Amaryllis: Graphing

One of the students gave us an amaryllis bulb and in January we planted it. It sprouted quickly and became our class pet. Using a meter stick, the students measured it daily—it grew that quickly—and posted the results on the chalkboard. The students then individually recorded the measurements on bar graphs on centimeter paper in their three-ring binders. I hadn't realized the plant would grow so quickly or so much. By the second week each student taped a second centimeter graph to the original and one above it to account for the rapid increase in height. By the third week the graphs had become cumbersome to fold into the students' notebooks. The following day I introduced the concept of scale.

I briefly explained the idea of scale to the fifth graders and let them come up with their own solutions for creating a scaled graph together in their groups. Meanwhile, I explained the concept of scale more carefully to the fourth graders because they had not had as many opportunities as the fifth graders to work with the scale concept. The fourth graders decided to scale down the plant with each centimeter on the graph representing five centimeters. They copied the dates of previous measurements and as they did this they reduced the size of the plant graph accordingly.

Inviting students (the fifth graders in this case) to come up with their own solutions for making the graph fit on one sheet allowed for one student to come up with a graph in which he recorded the amount the plant had grown every day, not the actual height. That graph focuses one's attention on change in height. Yes, it gives different information from the graph of the plant's height. Mathematically, the student had made a graph of first differences, which is related to the concept of first derivative as studied in calculus.

Another issue that came up as I reflected more closely on our graphing of the amaryllis was that using a bar graph for the growth of a plant was not as effective as using a line graph or simply plotting the points on a graph. We decided to explore this further by looking at different kinds of situations and deciding whether they could be better represented by a bar graph or by a line graph. This last type of graph also led us to discuss when to join the dots and when not to. For example, for the graph of the height of the plant it made sense to join the dots, but what about the graph of how many people are at home during the day[2]? Joining the dots in this situation would lead to saying things such as "There were 3.5 people at home at 7:15 A.M." Although students realized that statements such as this do not make sense, they were reluctant to not join the points. Nathan's comment "Joining the dots is like what we see in the newspaper or on TV; it makes us look more educated," made us smile, but it also reminded us of the influence that media can have.

Reflecting on the Year

As the year wound down and the weather became very hot and dry, the garden came to an end. We finished many of the weavings and were able to weave in yarn that was dyed by the fruit of a desert plant, the prickly pear. Our garden never did produce enough vegetables to be used for dye. The weavings, in their various stages of completion, each accompanied by a student's text, were placed on display in a glass case at the school. The students' work captured what had been a labor-intensive process lasting from November to March. The weavings looked authentic; they reflected the very process we had taken.

The students each took one plant home that was among the last we had planted (e.g., freesia and gladiolus). We took apart our enclosures and put them away, being careful to re-coil the chicken wire and tie it securely. I asked the children what surprised them the most about this experience and they were able to give articulate responses. Some of their comments suggested that it came as a surprise to them that "most of the things grew"; "the vegetables lived so long, especially through the winter"; "it was fun"; "the young broccoli

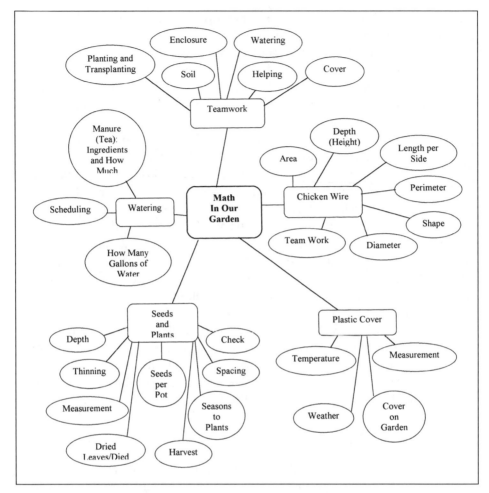

Figure 4–2. *Kate's Web of Mathematical Connections to the Garden*

tasted sweet!"; and "so many aphids fit on one leaf." With the help of parents, students, and project personnel, the experience provided a rich context for learning mathematics. We all came away understanding more about mathematics in our lives and the role it can play in a classroom. (For an example of students' thinking see Figures 4–2 and 4–3.)

　✷Negotiating curriculum with students is supported by my belief that students have the ability to teach themselves, and that is only possible by ongoing dialogue with the students throughout the year, to balance mandated curriculum and student interests. This dialogue develops into deep engagements in learning, in which students learn to think differently and are able to stay

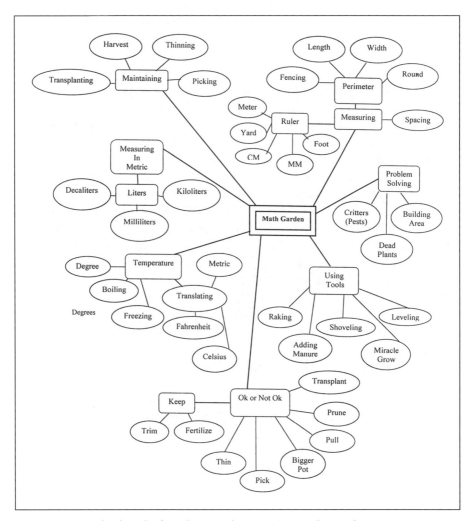

Figure 4–3.   *Nathan's Web of Mathematical Connections to the Garden*

with a project for a longer period of time. The students keep reapplying information that they have learned, especially in mathematics, over and over again in different and unfamiliar situations.

I believe that classrooms can teach children to stay focused even when the project or study becomes difficult; there are many ways we accomplish this. One of the parents told me that her son had a love-hate relationship with the garden, at times not caring if everything died off, but nonetheless wanting to go outside to check on it and see if the plants were okay. By staying with the project, though, this student could address mathematics through the eyes of someone who had successfully woven a small rug; incorporated a color pattern into the weaving; raised plants from seed and protected and nurtured them; and learned how to collaborate with his peers in situations that would have tried the patience of most adults.

Students who want to be in school, want to participate in the activities, and want to participate at a higher skill level are engaged learners; they drive the curriculum and are active participants in constructing their knowledge. Engaged learners are, therefore, what we would all hope our students will be.

Finally, the students needed an authentic reason to keep track of their information and/or class data. Jorge's experience in continuing to raise the tomatoes successfully, for example, was motivated by seeing his seedlings flourish and by the potential for generating capital for the classroom. His packed planting and careful watering forced us to think about how to get rid of the extra plants, and we came up with the idea of selling them. On the other hand, one of the most important parts of the experience for me was that Jorge was willing to write, with some help, a care sheet for growing tomatoes, which he gave to those students who purchased tomatoes during our plant sale.

As a teacher I realized that part of the reason that the unit continued for the year was that I kept introducing new problems/issues that had to be addressed if the garden were to keep going—pests (aphids), management issues (calendars), fertilizer (manure tea), replanting, and so on. So, while one aspect of the garden was deteriorating another part was beginning. There was a great deal of overlap and, in fact, the project in the students' eyes seemed continuous. Long-term projects, it seems, develop a commitment by the students. Further, because I continually fed the project with different aspects to make the experience broader and deeper, students became more and more engaged in the project, enabling them to call it their own.

Reflecting on the Mathematics (Marta Civil)

✱ Leslie's narrative reflects the importance of developing a curriculum theme unit that will build on the students' knowledge, experiences, and interests while at the same time help those students advance in their learning of academic mathematics. The narrative also attests to the level of commitment that this kind of work entails, not only on the part of the teacher but also on the part of students. The project was long-term, yet students persisted and were engaged throughout. Leslie spent a great deal of out-of-school time accessing and gathering necessary resources, developing activities, and constantly reflecting and revising her plans as needed, all without losing sight of an overarching framework. While Leslie had extensive gardening experience, she chose this theme in part because of the funds of knowledge of many of her students and their families.

Leslie actively listened to her students' voices and, in turn, found out about their needs and their desires as learners. This narrative sheds some light on questions that we have been pondering here and elsewhere: What might a learning environment look like if we tried to develop more participation-oriented approaches toward the learning of mathematics similar to what these and other students experience in their out-of-school lives? What might be the implications for the mathematical education of students if we took their lived experiences and backgrounds as resources for learning in the classroom? As an aside, Leslie's own motivation for being in project BRIDGE, for example, was to explore whether "rigorous" mathematics (e.g., study of perimeter and area) could be developed from everyday mathematics (e.g., the chicken wire dilemma).

These are key issues in our project activities. As we strive to address the subject of contextualizing the learning of mathematics, we are faced with what we perceive as tensions between "formal" mathematics and "informal" mathematics, or between everyday mathematics and academic mathematics. These tensions play themselves out at different levels. For example, at one level we ask: Will students and their parents and teachers view informal mathematics as real mathematics? And on the other hand, at yet another level, we ask ourselves: As the teacher works on moving students from the informal to the more academic, how do we ensure that the classroom discourse and the tasks remain engaging for all students?

The gardening theme gives us an example in which these potential tensions between everyday mathematics and academic mathematics are actually strengths toward the learning of mathematics in a school. Leslie used a real-life problem—the need to enlarge the garden enclosures using the very same fencing material—to take her students into a wonderful exploration of maximizing the area of shapes with a fixed perimeter. From a more practical point of view (that is, for their more immediate needs), the children did not "need" this mathematical exploration: they had easily enlarged their gardens by trial and error, moving around the chicken wire. Yet, the students eagerly engaged in a serious exploration of academic mathematics through their artificial garden enclosures made out of string.

This approach to the learning of mathematics, which allows students to come up with their own ideas, test them, revise them, and discuss them, is consistent with Leslie's more holistic views of teaching and learning. Such an approach meets many challenges and requires a rather courageous teacher, willing to take the risk of letting go of control as the authority figure and letting students go in directions that may be mathematically unfamiliar to all involved. For example, in the string activity, one of the students used different size bits of sponge to find the area of her shape. This is problematic, as one cannot say "The area is _____ sponge units," since the pieces were of varying sizes. Also, when Leslie first saw the amaryllis graph of first differences, she realized that she did not know what it meant and was unsure about what to do with it.

How can teachers assess the mathematical validity of students' ideas? Teachers such as Leslie manage to do so through a combination of their own knowledge and understanding of mathematics and an intellectual curiosity that pushes them to learn more about mathematics as well as locate and seek out the support that they find in the collaborative structure of the project's study group meetings. Following students' mathematical paths is indeed no easy task. These teachers not only do that but also remain on the lookout for mathematical opportunities in everyday practices.

In our project work, a key challenge has been the uncovering of mathematics in everyday life situations. By this we have meant going beyond a description of more or less superficial uses of mathematics in everyday situations. For participating teacher-researchers, a familiarity with the household practices themselves, as in the case of Leslie's knowledge about gardening, has been quite beneficial. This certainly raises implications for the classroom in the form of questions, among them: To what extent can a teacher develop mathematically rich experiences that are grounded in practices with which she or he is not familiar? And even if one is familiar with the practices, how does one go about examining the mathematics embedded within them? How do our views about what we count as being and knowing mathematics affect what we will see in everyday practices?

These are some of the questions that we are still considering as we work on connecting the household experiences with school mathematics. By turning our attention to household knowledge we were able to find a way to develop a classroom learning environment that was mathematically rich while using activities that were meaningful and authentic to the children.

Notes

1. Leslie and Marta have been working collaboratively on project BRIDGE (Linking Home and School: A Bridge to the Many Faces of Mathematics) since 1996. Leslie has continued her growth in mathematics by taking some of Marta's courses at the University and by attending inservices offered by Tucson Unified School District.

2. This activity was adapted from the Investigation in Number, Data, and Space (TERC) series.

5

The Sound of Drums[1]

FAITH R. CONANT, ANN ROSEBERY,
BETH WARREN & JOSIANE HUDICOURT-BARNES

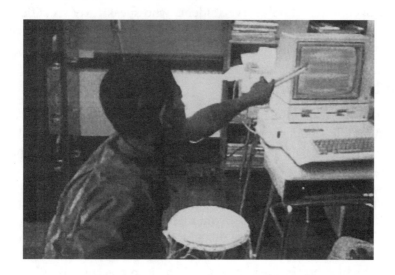

It is time for science. In the corner of the classroom, four Haitian middle school students cluster around an African-style drum and a computer. The boys are using the computer to analyze the sounds of a traditional Haitian drum rhythm. Jean picks up the microphone that is attached to the computer and holds it over the drumhead. Paul plays a series of drum strokes. The boys watch the computer screen as a waveform for each sound appears. Jean hits a key on the keyboard to freeze the waveform for a particular drum stroke. He prints the screen display so it can be included in a poster the boys are making that shows differences in the tones produced by different kinds of strokes on the drum. While Jean is busy with the computer, Manuel holds up a paper

51

with a waveform the boys printed previously. He asks Paul which stroke of the drum rhythm the waveform represents so he can label it for their poster. Paul recognizes the waveform and explains where the drummer's hand hits the drumhead to produce it and the kind of sound that results.

Background

This scene is from Josiane Hudicourt-Barnes' seventh/eighth-grade class in the Haitian Creole bilingual program in Cambridge, Massachusetts. Cambridge is a culturally, linguistically, and socioeconomically diverse city. The Cambridge public schools serve students who speak forty-six different languages in the community; the conversations reported here have been translated from Haitian Creole into English.

Problematic Beginnings

Josiane set out to teach her students a unit on sound, at the time a standard topic in middle school science in the district. She began with a typical instructional activity: to establish a set of common terms to use to describe pitch and volume. She put a two-by-two matrix on the board and labeled the rows with the Creole words for *loud* and *soft* and the columns with the Creole words for *high-pitched* and *low-pitched*. Then she dropped a number of objects (a basketball, paper clips, a book, etc.) from a fixed height and asked the students to think about the sound each one made as it hit the floor. Was it high-pitched and soft? Low-pitched and loud? High-pitched and loud? According to its sound, in which box in the matrix should a given object be listed?

To Josiane's surprise, the students did not agree on the descriptions of the sounds. One student described the sound a basketball made as it hit the floor as high-pitched and loud, another described it as low-pitched and loud, and still another described it as loud and soft. This happened with several objects. Caught off guard, Josiane tried explaining the qualities of pitch and volume to her students. But as she talked, she realized that Creole terms for sound, like their English counterparts, are often ambiguous and can carry more than one meaning. The Creole word for *deep* or *low-pitched* is *gwo,* but gwo can also mean big and loud. The Creole word for *high-pitched* is *fen* but fen can also mean small and quiet. This is analogous to the words *high* and *low* in English, which can describe both volume and pitch. Josiane realized that untangling pitch and volume, both acoustically and linguistically, was going to be harder for her and her students than she had anticipated.

The next day, Josiane introduced computer software specifically designed to support the study of sound. The software, Microcomputer-Based

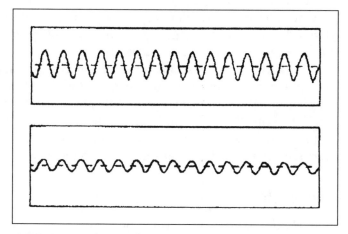

Figure 5–1.   *MBL-Generated Waves for Sounds Produced by a Tuning Fork at Different Volumes, Louder (top) and Softer (bottom)*

Laboratory Sound (MBL), creates a screen display in the form of sound waves for any sound made into a specially adapted microphone (see Figure 5–1). Josiane hoped MBL would help her students learn to distinguish features of sound in a way more characteristic of scientific discourse by allowing them to focus on data and inscriptions and move them away from simple arguments over their individual perceptions in ungrounded terms. She wanted them to be able to use the MBL sound wave inscriptions as a resource to analyze and compare different kinds of sounds.

Josiane pointed to two contrasting waveforms on the computer screen, representing sounds made by the same tuning fork at different volumes.

Students: Yes. No. [They count the number of wave crests together]

Josiane: Are there the same number of mountains?

Students: Yes!

Josiane: But those mountains are taller. What do you think the height means?

Students: Pitch! Volume!

Student: The one on top is bigger.

Josiane: It's bigger. So what does that show?

Student: Size.

Student: Louder.

Student: Volume.

Student: Pitch.

Many of even the most vocal students in the class were understandably unsure of how to interpret Josiane's questions and the MBL displays. MBL represented sound consistently, but the significance of its representations had to be negotiated. A mountain's bigness certainly shows "size." It is an achievement to see mountains in terms of *sound,* however, especially when the sound represented is no longer audible. Despite Josiane's adoption of the students' term "mountains" for the waveforms' crests, and the students' hopeful attempts to use her terms "volume" and "pitch," both she and the students struggled in their attempts to reach an agreement with one another about what they were seeing and saying about sound and sound waves.

A New Approach

As she thought about the problems she and her students were encountering, Josiane felt a need to anchor their learning and her instruction in aspects of sound with which they were already familiar. She wanted to create an instructional context that would allow the students to build on what they already knew about sound. As it happened, the students had been recently recruited to play Haitian drum rhythms as accompaniment to a school play that depicted life in the Caribbean. To prepare for the play, the students would work with a local drummaker to build three African-style drums. They would also apprentice to a Haitian master drummer to learn traditional Haitian drum rhythms.

Josiane organized the students into small groups. One group of boys, Paul, Manuel, Marc, and Jean, took responsibility for making a poster showing the different kinds of drum strokes they were learning for the music in the play. They used MBL to generate and print waveforms for the different strokes. At one point, Paul suggested that they create a waveform for a drum stroke made with a stick, and one for a drum stroke made with a hand in the center of the drum. First, Paul played a stick stroke that Jean froze on the computer screen and printed (see Figure 5–2). Paul then played the entire rhythm through several times, expecting Jean to freeze one of the hand strokes (as in Figure 5–3). Instead, Jean unintentionally froze the waveform for a second stick stroke (see Figure 5–4). Comparing the waveforms (Figures 5–2 and 5–4), Paul protested, "But they're both sticks!" He had learned that the waveform for the sound made by a stick stroke should look different from the waveform for a sound made by a hand stroke. He was beginning to recognize how differences in sound were encoded in the sound waveforms.

According to Haitian custom, the students had dubbed the traditional rhythm they were learning with words. This practice, with roots in West Africa, makes it possible to refer to individual drum strokes by "name," with-

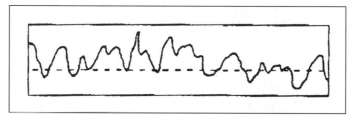

Figure 5–2. *Drawing of MBL-Generated Wave of a Drum Stroke Made by a Stick*

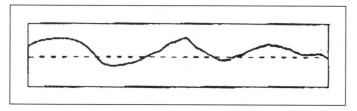

Figure 5–3. *Drawing of MBL-Generated Waveform of a Drum Stroke Made by Hand*

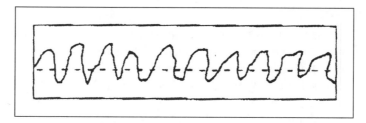

Figure 5–4. *Drawing of MBL-Generated Wave of Another Stick Drum Stroke*

out a lengthy description of the technique used to produce them. Each sylla-ble of a word phrase stands for one stroke on the drum. Among themselves, the boys dubbed their rhythm with the phrase "Leta bouda kalimet." As their investigation progressed, the boys began to use the dubbing convention as a resource in their learning. In the following exchange, they used it to con-strain a claim of what a particular inscription represented. Jean claimed that a given waveform inscription represented three drummed strokes (repre-sented by "kalimet"), while Manuel argued that it should represent only one (such as "ka").

Faith: What are they [Pointing to the waveform inscriptions]?

Manuel: It's a printout that—the sounds we got from the drum, they recorded the sound, it appeared on the computer, these—[Addressing Jean] (do you know) which these [waveform inscriptions] were? These two.

Jean: [Indicating one waveform] That is "kalimet." [Indicating a second wave-
form] That is a "bouda."

Manuel: [Checking and pointing to one waveform] This is "le"? This is "ka"? And
this [Pointing to the second waveform]?

Jean: This one's "kalimet."

Manuel: No, no, no. You can't say that. It should be a single one, only one.

Having been intimately involved with the repeated production of sound
wave inscriptions, Manuel had learned that although a single sound wave is
made up of many troughs and peaks ("mountains"), each waveform in the
thirty-millisecond MBL window represents only one drummed stroke or a
single syllable of the dubbed words. In arguing this point with Jean, Manuel
enforced an interpretative convention of the inscription he had learned from
his group's work in collecting sound waves.

The Inscription Presentation

In creating their poster (see Figure 5–5), the boys juxtaposed inscriptions of
the different drum strokes used in the rhythm they had learned for the play.
In four columns from left to right, the poster shows (1) each syllable of the
dubbed phrase "Leta manje twòp patat" ("The arrogant kid eats too many
sweet potatoes"); (2) the sound wave inscription of the drum stroke associated with each syllable; (3) for each syllable, an aerial-view drawing of the
hand positions and techniques involved in producing the sound on the drum;
and (4) an explanation of how each stroke was made on the drum.

Before the play, Paul, Manuel, Marc, and Jean presented their poster to
the class. One student, Kelvin, interpreted their presentation and inscriptions
as a claim about "the way the things really are," and challenged them to prove
to him that the representations on the poster could be taken as the sounds
themselves.

Kelvin: If, if , if that's the way things are, they have to go do it again so I can see if
that's the way the things really are.

Student: Oh!

Teacher: You want them to play it now into the computer?

Before he would accept the inscriptions in front of him in lieu of "the
things" themselves (i.e., the sounds of the drum strokes), Kelvin insisted that
the results be repeated. With her question, Josiane underscored Kelvin's insis-
tence on this form of proof. While the boys had presented the poster as a

Leta manje twòp patat

Sylab / Syllable	Sound wave / Lanm son	Hands Position / Pozisyon men	Esplikasyon / esplikasyon
Le		Right Hand	Premye son sa se le ou frape men ou nan mitan an bwi a fè 'le'
ta		Right 2nd / Left Hand	Dezyem son sa se lè ou mele men ou sou kote tanbou a epi ou frape li epi li fè 'Ta'
man		Right Hand	Son sa se lè ou frape men dwat ou nan mitan tanbou a li fè man.
jè		Left 2nd	Son sa se lè ou frape men goch ou sou goch la li fè je.
twòp		Left Hand	Son sa se lè ou frape men goch ou sou kote goch la li fe twop.
Pa		Left Hand	Son sa se lè ou frape men goch sou kote tanbou a li fè pa.
tat		Right Hand	Son sa se lè ou frape men ou nan mitan an net li ule di Psit

Figure 5–5. *Students' Poster Representing Drum Strokes from a Traditional Haitian Rhyme, Which the Students Dubbed with the Words "Leta Manje Twòp Patat," "The arrogant kid eats too many sweet potatoes."*

finished product, Kelvin's challenge located it in a different field, one of claims, questions, and proof. In this way, the boys' work was as much about basic properties of sound as it was about the status of inscriptions as claims about "the way the things really are." Typically in school, the significance of inscriptions as contestable claims about the world, so central to the work of scientific communities, is often unrecognized.

In a class discussion after the play, Marc showed what his work with drums and MBL had helped him learn about sound. He illustrated for the class his understanding of the term *bass* by drawing contrasting sound waves with a ratio of wavelengths consistent with computer-generated inscriptions for low- and high-pitched drum sounds. The bass wave had fewer and wider peaks than the nonbass wave. Marc's drawing demonstrated to Josiane that he had linked the everyday term *bass* to specific features of sound waveforms. He had effectively translated his own experience into a symbolic language of science. Here, in contrast to the earlier demonstration with tuning forks, Josiane and her student were clearly understanding one another and sharing a sense of the uses and conventions of inscriptions. This discussion, the earlier one of the boys' poster, and others that occurred during the course of the unit convinced her that the boys' work with drums and MBL had enriched their understanding of aspects of pitch and volume and given them firsthand experience with how these features are represented, interpreted, and used in science.

Conclusion

From a scientific perspective, what did the students learn? Their explorations with drums and MBL enriched their understanding of various aspects of sound and enabled them to talk to one another and to their teacher in grounded ways about particular features of pitch and volume. In addition, they learned how to interpret various symbolic features of sound wave inscriptions. They also had experience with the ways in which such inscriptions are used in science to transform claims into facts. In this light, the boys' learning was as much about the use of inscriptions in science as about distinctions in the characterization of sound.

The boys also gained a deeper understanding of drums and drumming from their apprenticeships to a drummaker and a master drummer. They learned about the design and component parts of traditional African drums, how to build them, how to stretch the skins for the drumheads, how to adjust the pegs to tune the drums, and the like. They learned traditional Haitian drumming rhythms and performed them in the school play. They also mastered conventions for dubbing rhythms with word phrases to refer to particular drum strokes.

We do not mean to suggest that the students' learning about sound and learning about drums were separate activities governed by a scientific perspective in the first case and a musical perspective in the second, or that drumming simply provided a familiar, motivating context for the scientific study of sound. Rather, we want to stress the *interconnectedness* of the science of sound and the students' knowledge of drum rhythms and how students' funds of knowledge could be used dynamically in support of learning.

We wish to make an additional point about drums as the object of investigation. The choice of drums was serendipitous, yet clearly powerful. At the time Josiane's students were asked to drum for the school play, she did not foresee the connection to the sound unit. We feel it would be a mistake to read this as a story of culturally sensitive instruction, that is, of an instance of simply identifying a familiar context on which to overlay academic learning. Rather, drumming, MBL, and the students' *own* questions and intentions worked together to create a provocative, fertile environment for learning about sound and about drum rhythms. It was the conceptual connections between the discourse world of drums and that of the science of sound—connections created by the students—that mattered to Josiane and that were crucial to her students' learning. Josiane's imaginative insight lay in recognizing that she could create an instructional space that was at once a technical one for learning how to produce a variety of drum sounds and a scientific one for learning about features of sound.

The final form of the sound investigation depended on Josiane's openness to listening to what her students were saying (Ball 1997; Ballenger 1997, 1999; Duckworth 1987; Gallas 1995; Paley 1986; Rosebery 1998; Warren 1998). We do not think that sharing a language or a nationality with students in and of itself enables a teacher to develop instructional contexts that truly interweave students' ways of knowing with academic ways of knowing. Instead, good teaching is based, at least in part, on attending to the particular ways children make sense of things, to their ideas about the world, and on a commitment to looking for ways to build on the deep connections between the children's ideas and ways of knowing and those of science. Children's ideas, if taken seriously, will inevitably challenge and enrich a teacher's understanding of and assumptions about science, about what children can and cannot learn, and about pedagogical possibilities.

Note

1. The writing of this chapter was supported by the Center for Research on Education, Diversity, and Excellence, University of California–Santa Cruz, Educational Research and Development Centers Program, PR/Award Number R306A60001, as administered by the Office of Educational Research and Improvement, U.S. Department of Education. The data on which this chapter is based were collected under the Innovative Approaches Research Project, contract No. 300-87-0131, U.S. Department of Education, Office of Bilingual Education and Minority Language Affairs.

References

Ball, D. 1997. "What Do Students Know? Facing Challenges of Distance, Context, and Desire in Trying to Hear Children." In *International Handbook on Teaching and Teaching, 2*, ed. T. Biddle, T. Goodman, & I. Goodson, 769–817. Dordrecht, Netherlands: Kluwer Press.

Ballenger, C. 1997. "Social Identities, Moral Narratives, Scientific Argumentation: Science Talk in a Bilingual Classroom." *Language and Education* 11 (1): 1–13.

———. 1999. *Teaching Other People's Children: Literacy and Learning in a Bilingual Classroom.* New York: Teachers College Press.

Conant, F. 1996. "Leta Manje Twòp Patat: Drums in the Science Lab." *Hands On!* 19 (1): 7–10.

Duckworth, E. 1987. *The Having of Wonderful Ideas.* New York: Teachers College Press.

Gallas, K. 1995. *Talking Their Way into Science: Hearing Children's Questions and Theories, Responding with Curricula.* New York: Teachers College Press.

Latour, B., & S. Woolgar. 1986. *Laboratory Life: The Social Construction of Scientific Facts.* Princeton, NJ: Princeton University Press.

Paley, V. 1986. "On Listening to What the Children Say." *Harvard Educational Review* 56 (2): 122–31.

Rosebery, A. 1998. "Investigating a Teacher's Questions Through Video." In *Boats, Balloons, and Classroom Video: Science Teaching as Inquiry,* ed. A. S. Rosebery & B. Warren, 73–80. Portsmouth, NH: Heinemann.

Rosebery, A., B. Warren, & F. Conant. 1992. "Appropriating Scientific Discourse: Findings from Language Minority Classrooms." *The Journal of the Learning Sciences* 2 (1): 61–94.

Rosebery, A., B. Warren, F. Conant, & J. Hudicourt-Barnes. 1992. "Scientific Sense-Making in Bilingual Education." *Hands On!* 15 (1): 1, 16–19.

Warren, B. 1998. "'That's Another Meaning for Volume Then, for Me': On Learning from What Children Say." In *Boats, Balloons, and Classroom Video: Science Teaching as Inquiry,* ed. A. S. Rosebery & B. Warren, 51–59. Portsmouth, NH: Heinemann.

Warren, B., & M. Ogonowski. (n.d.). *From Knowledge to Knowing: An Inquiry into Teacher Learning in Science.* Center for the Development of Teaching Paper Series. Newton, MA: Education Development Center. In press.

Warren, B., & A. Rosebery. 1995. "Equity in the Future Tense: Redefining Relationships Among Teachers, Students, and Science in Linguistic Minority Classrooms." In *New Directions for Equity in Mathematics Education,* ed. W. Secada, E. Fennema, & L. Adajian, 289–328. New York: Cambridge University Press.

———. 1996. "'This Question Is Just Too, Too, Easy!' Students' Perspectives on Accountability in Science." In *Innovations in Learning: New Environments for Education,* ed. L. Schauble & R. Glaser, 97–125. Mahwah, NJ: Erlbaum.

6
Preschool Science

*Contextualizing Curriculum
with Children's Questions and Family Stories*

MAUREEN CALLANAN, PILAR COTO, LIGIA MIRANDA,
ANNE STRIFFLER, JIM ALLEN, CHERIE CRANDALL
& COLLEEN MURPHY

Photo by Jon Kersey

Pilar and her preschool group gathered to talk about the eggs that were keeping warm in the incubator. In their discussion a question came up: "Where's the mommy chicken? If there is no mommy, who will take care of the little chicks when they hatch?" Pilar reports that in the conversation that followed, the group came up with an answer: "We will all be the mommies; we will take care of the chicks." Over the next weeks, the children, their teachers, and

61

their families took their roles as caregivers very seriously. The students' consensus on this idea, and their joint activity in carrying it out, illustrate several ways that curriculum can be contextualized in the lives of young children.

Why raise chicks? There were several reasons that Pilar and her colleagues decided on this project at this time. Raising chicks fit the general theme of springtime, it would provide an opportunity for children to consider familiar things—eggs—from a new perspective, and it was a hands-on project with potentially rich thematic connections to books, songs, and other projects. Most important, the project would foster a deep focus on the processes of development that are common to all living things. The staff believed that the opportunity to observe the process of birth and development would be very valuable because it would help children understand their own experiences of growth and change and their similarity to all living things. Although preschool teachers might prefer to use different terminology to describe it, one might say that this was a life science project with the goals of expanding children's understanding of biological organisms and linking that science knowledge to other disciplines, including literacy, art, music, and mathematics.

Although they were interested in the potential depth of this topic, the teachers were cautious about the practical issues that they would need to overcome. Hatching eggs would take a great deal of dedication on their part, and they knew the risk of disappointment if the eggs did not develop properly. (Some had had experiences with "hard-boiled eggs" in other classrooms.) One teacher, Ligia, made a personal investment in a high-quality incubator and agreed to adopt the chicks when they were too big to stay at school. Beyond their commitment to carefully prepare the project, these teachers also had a commitment to child-centered and contextualized curriculum. Their approach is consistent with the goals of "developmentally appropriate practice" and "integrated curriculum" as outlined by the National Association for the Education of Young Children (NAEYC) (see Bredekamp 1987; Hart, Burts, & Charlesworth 1997). The point of this chapter is not to suggest that raising chicks is a novel project for preschoolers. Instead, this project is presented here as a concrete illustration of how a group of teachers put this approach into practice and of how their approach made it possible for the project to evolve in ways that even the teachers had not anticipated.

As you will see, teachers in this preschool contextualize the curriculum in several of the ways addressed in Chapter One: (1) by allowing children to initiate curriculum; (2) by paying special attention to children's questions as a way to gauge their interest, curiosity, and understanding; and (3) by inviting parents to share family stories, including conversations children have at home about the topics being studied at school. In addition, the staff and board of directors of this preschool are committed to two other distinctive features in the philosophy that are also relevant to contextualized instruction: (4) the school has an antibias philosophy (see Derman-Sparks & the ABC Task Force 1989), which celebrates diversity through creating an inclusive environment for children and families of all backgrounds and family structures; and (5) the school has adopted a bilingual approach to instruction, which means that there is a fluent Spanish-speaking (fully qualified) teacher present at all times, and there is a commitment to Spanish language instruction in order to benefit both first and second language learners. Each of these five features of contextualized instruction will be discussed in this chapter, through the example of the chick-raising unit, as well as another life science unit that focused on snakes.

Child-Initiated Curriculum

The idea for the chick-hatching project ultimately came from the children themselves. Over a period of several months, the children had shown a great deal of interest in learning about different kinds of animals. One child, Joaquín, had single-handedly initiated a study of snakes by bringing books, pets, and information from home. Pilar noticed that the other children were also becoming intrigued with snakes because of this child's interest. She opened up time to spend on a snake theme. In this unit, Pilar reports, "We learned together. I openly shared that I was not a snake expert, even though I was the teacher." Pilar often turned to Joaquín, the class "snake expert," for answers to questions that she or others were curious about. She stepped back, allowing much of the learning to be entirely child-directed. She saw her role as enabling children to keep going by encouraging them and by introducing projects, books, and songs that were relevant to their interests. She depended on the children to let her know when they were satisfied with what they had learned about snakes; for example, she waited until the children stopped asking questions before assuming that they were ready to move on to a new topic.

The children were intrigued by snakes' bodies, their movement, and their eating habits. They explored these issues with their own bodies by slithering on the floor. Joaquín suggested that they tuck their hands and arms inside their shirts, because "snakes do not have hands." They closed their eyes while slithering, and tried smelling with their tongues. Pilar suggested a project of making rattles out of cardboard containers and beans. The children expanded on this idea by asking her to tie the rattles around their ankles so they could shake them while slithering.

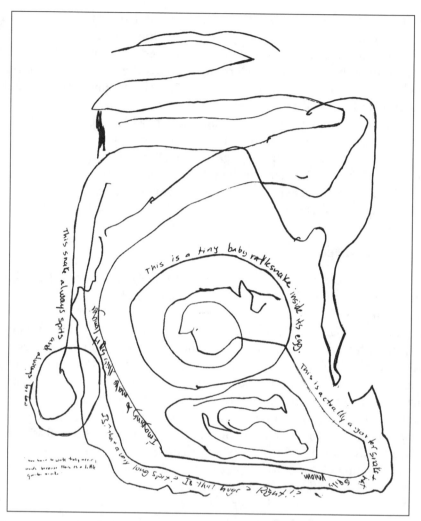

Figure 6–1. *A Baby Rattlesnake Inside Its Egg*

The children were mesmerized by descriptions of snakes' eating habits, such as swallowing meals whole and opening their jaws to suit the size of their prey. The children in Pilar's group even incorporated their fascination with snakes into the school's production of "The Wizard of Oz." Children decided on their own parts in the play, and this group chose to be snakes who slithered across the yellow brick road.

The teachers used the snake theme to bring in more academic curriculum as well. Together, the children drew an anaconda on large graph paper,

Figure 6–2. *Swarm of Diamondback Rattlesnakes*

estimating its relative size by applying what they had learned in books. They learned new vocabulary words such as *constricts, anaconda, prey, venom,* and *digest.* They learned many facts about digestion and life cycles. Perhaps most important, they acted like scientists, learning through observation, discovery, and asking and answering questions on their own.

The children's engagement in this topic, which lasted for many weeks, encouraged the teachers to focus on other animals. In many ways the chick unit followed from this focus on snakes.

Children's (and Teachers') Questions

Children's questions are an important focus for the teachers in this preschool. Pilar and the other teachers pay very special attention to the questions that children ask, and they try to resist the authority role of providing answers. Instead, they try to treat children's questions as open invitations for the whole group to engage in a process of deeper inquiry. With their own questions as well, these teachers discuss their struggle to get away from the more traditional habits of asking children questions as a way to get the "right" answers. They try to model the activity of inquiry by asking questions that are open-ended and invite exploration.

The question at the beginning of the chapter—"Where's the mommy chicken?"—became a very important focus for the rest of the egg-hatching unit. The teachers saw in this question how important the idea of nurturance was for the children. The children raised this issue in other ways, for example, quoting phrases from a song they had learned, "Los Pollitos," to describe how they would "put the chicks under [their] armpits." Pilar noticed that children from different family structures seemed especially interested in the idea that young creatures can be cared for by all types of people. It was also notable that none of the children seemed to complain about boys being considered mommies for the chicks. Pilar felt that they had agreed to share the role of mommy for these chicks and they accepted this unusual arrangement as one type of family.

Many of the children's questions about chickens and other birds were expressed and explored in the context of their activities. "What do chickens do?" became the focus of much of the free play outside in the yard. Children— both boys and girls—were often spotted making nests in the sand, pretending to sit on their own eggs, and fluttering, because "chickens don't really fly." Instead of the usual superhero play, teachers noted a great deal of fantasy play about hawks swooping down, chasing other birds, and so on. The scientific facts that children were learning through books and conversation, and the questions that they were wondering about were being embodied in their fantasy play. The child who was interested in snakes said, "Do you know what would happen if we put a boa in that incubator? He'd eat all those chickens!"

Because they were learning along with the children, the teachers found that they had authentic questions of their own. For example, when the eggs began to hatch, they found that they were surprised at how long it took. "Should it really take this long for the chicks to make their way out of the egg?" Teachers found themselves looking in books to find answers to their own questions about the process as the birds emerged from the eggs. Im-

Figure 6–3. *Chicks When They Hatch Out of the Incubator*

mersed as they were in the events that were unfolding, these questions and their answers took on meaning for the teachers as well as the children. Parents and children created a new daily ritual—spending more and more time in the classroom as they paid close attention to the dramatic changes in the incubator. Becoming engaged by their own questions, teachers modeled for children a process of discovery, and stayed away from the more traditional role of being experts who already knew the answers. This approach to science learning is precisely what is recommended by both the American Association for the Advancement of Science and the National Academy of Science's National Research Council (see Lind 1997).

The teachers also used questions in more planful ways in order to encourage children to understand phenomena from new perspectives. One day Anne asked, "What does it look like to be inside an egg?" She provided egg-shaped pieces of paper, and children drew pictures and told the teacher about them. One little girl drew a little chick and told a story that the teacher wrote down (Figure 6–4): "Once upon a time, I lived in an egg . . . Nobody could see me. My mommy duck kept the egg warm. My mom saved food for me when I get out. It was big inside my egg. I was really wet. When I came out, I was all tired. I flopped down and took a rest. When I dried off, I was all fluffy! The end." Another child drew a picture of a baby hawk (Figure 6–5), saying, "It's fleshy inside the egg. I crack out with my beak. I eat meat that my Mom gets." Anne's question opened up possibilities and perspectives for the children rather than closing in on a single answer. It invited children to do what scientists often do: imagine oneself inside a scientific phenomenon and begin to understand it in a personal way.

once upon a time, I lived in an egg...
Nobody could see me. My mommy duck kept
the egg warm. My mom saved food for me when
I get out. It was big inside my egg. I was
really wet. When I came out, I was all tired.
I flopped down and took a rest. When I dried
off, I was all fluffy !!

The End

Story by I. sobel

Figure 6–4. *Baby Duck Story*

The chicks' arrival allowed many new questions to be asked and answered. Anne embedded some mathematics in the activities with the chicks, asking the question "How much do the chicks weigh?"

First, they weighed several chicks, noticing that different birds weighed different amounts. Anne then asked children to suggest objects around the class room that might weigh the same amount as a chick. When they had some objects ready, she chose one of the chicks, placed it on one side of a two-pan scale, and together they observed what happened when different objects were placed on the other side of the scale. In the end, it was a Lego person that came closest to the chick's weight. This was an exercise that introduced new terminology (e.g., *ounces*), as well as mathematical concepts such as comparing the relative size of different birds, and noticing how weight relates to other physical features.

Ligia had promised from the beginning that she would take the chicks to live at her house when they were too big to stay at school. After several weeks, she brought them back for a visit. There was a flurry of excitement when the children and the chickens greeted one another. New questions emerged as the children focused on the many ways the chicks had changed. "Why are they flapping their wings so hard and making sand get on their bodies?" Ligia an-

Figure 6–5. *A Baby Hawk Inside Its Egg*

swered that they were cleaning their feathers. Even though she would often encourage children to find their own answers, there are times when it feels right to a teacher to answer a child's question with some information that she knows.

One boy asked, "I wonder how they got white?" The teachers capitalized on these questions, not only by talking about how the chicks had changed into chickens but also by talking about the changes that occur as children grow into adults. Another child asked, "Where did those chickens come from?" When he understood that these were the same little chicks that he had helped to raise, he said, "Where are the black ones?" Ligia suggested that he look closely and try to guess which ones used to be black. He guessed, "Maybe the speckled ones." Some children compared changes in the chicks with changes that people go through as they grow. Just as the teachers had hoped, by raising the chicks, the children had not only learned a great deal about development but had also found ways to apply their knowledge to their understanding of their own growth and development. At the same time, the children's own focus on nurturance carried through.

Home-School Connections

Teachers' connections with parents enrich their understanding of their students and help them create rich and supportive learning environments. As Moll and González (1994) have pointed out, parents possess funds of knowledge that can be utilized to great benefit in the classroom. Contextualizing classroom instruction by making connections to children's community and cultural experiences is an essential way to make curriculum meaningful for children (Tharp 1997). Another way for teachers to contextualize instruction is to communicate with parents regarding children's interests. Finding out about conversations at home may inform teachers about how children are understanding the topics being studied at school.

The theme of nurturing came up again in conversations between teachers and parents when parents were dropping off or picking up their children. One parent related a story about her own experiences raising a chick in her classroom when she was a child. She recalled going on a field trip to the farm where the chick had been adopted, seeing a sea of chickens, and then noticing one chicken leaving the crowd to walk directly over to the group of children that had raised it. The emotion in this story was striking. Many parents showed their own fascination with the process, checking on the eggs each time they came to the school and looking for signs of change. Other parents brought in books or pets from home. Through these family connections, the project was further contextualized in children's lives.

Parents often shared stories from home, which helped teachers understand more about how individual children were learning and responding to the project. One child's mother reported a change that she attributed to the chick raising. This child had always been kind but had not extended that kindness to insects. In fact, he had sometimes smashed insects when he saw them on the ground. When the chicks were about one week old, the mother observed the following: The child picked up a ladybug and placed it on his open palm, saying, "Hi, ladybug! Are you having a good Saturday? Do you want to be a mama some day?" His mother asked, "How do you know that it's a female?" He replied, "Because it has spots. Males have no spots." Whether or not this was correct, this child was clearly trying out ways to classify animals. Turning his attention back to the ladybug, he said, "I hope that you have a really nice day, ladybug. And that you have lots of babies." As the ladybug flew away, he added, "Have a nice life, ladybug, and I love you always." This example shows a child extending new feelings of nurturance and caring to small creatures that he had not previously treated in this way. Parents are in an excellent position to recognize such examples as representing change in their children's attitudes; knowing about these examples helps teachers see the ways that their curriculum choices are affecting individual children. This example also showed teachers that this child was recognizing similarities between the chicks in the classroom and other kinds of living creatures, and that he was thinking about gender differences within a species, about life cycles and development, and about reproduction. This is a rich array of scientific topics.

Inclusive Atmosphere

Because of their commitment to antibias curriculum, the teachers have a goal of creating a classroom where all children feel included. The antibias curriculum approach involves going beyond a focus on foods and holidays of other cultures. Instead, this approach encourages children and teachers to develop skills for recognizing and counteracting bias (Derman-Sparks & the ABC Task Force 1989). One way to do this is for teachers to be aware of the ways that some children may feel left out.

One mother, who was a lesbian parent, expressed a profound appreciation for the chick-raising project. She commented that the discussions children were having about the incubator and about who would care for the chicks left open possibilities for different types of family structures as well as different kinds of birth stories. The fact that the children and teachers would be the caregivers, for example, might be a welcome variation from the stereotypical two-parent family for her child as well as for children from one-parent families and adoptive families. The teachers had not anticipated this reaction, but they saw it as a positive aspect of the project, and they built on this mother's comment by focusing further on the fact that babies can be raised in different ways and children can come from all types of families.

One way that antibias curriculum can teach tolerance is by helping children and teachers recognize their own assumptions and realize that not all of them are shared by others. In the chick project, the focus on alternative ways to care for young creatures may have helped children see diversity as a positive thing.

Bilingual Emphasis

The emphasis on a bilingual environment in this preschool is based in the beliefs that children's home languages must be valued and supported and that it is beneficial for all children to be exposed to a second language at a young age.

Spanish is used in the context of real activity, not in the context of direct translation or didactic instruction, consistent with a "two-way immersion" approach (Christian 1996; Lindholm 1995). For example, children learned the Spanish song "Los Pollitos" as part of the chick-hatching unit. They commented with excitement that "even chicks can speak Spanish" because the chicks in the song say "pío, pío" instead of "peep, peep." Children who are being exposed to Spanish as a second language are more likely to learn words and phrases that are meaningful and important to them. Embedding Spanish language in the chick-hatching project may be thought of as yet another example of integrated curriculum.

LOS POLLITOS	THE BABY CHICKS
Los pollitos dicen	The baby chicks are singing
Pío, pío, pío.	Pío, pío, pío.
Cuando tienen hambre,	Mama we are hungry
Cuando tienen frío.	Mama we are cold.
La gallina busca	Mama looks for wheat
El maíz y el trigo	Mama looks for corn.
Les de la comida	Mama feeds them dinner
Y les presta abrigo.	Mama keeps them warm.
Bajo sus dos alas	Under mama's wings
Acurrucaditos	sleeping in the hay
Hasta el otra día	baby chicks all huddle
Duermen los pollitos	until the next day.

For children who are learning English as a second language, it is difficult to engage in intellectual inquiry if many of the words being used are not familiar to them. For this reason, the staff in this school has made a commitment to conduct Spanish circle times, when topics such as hatching are discussed in the same depth of meaning as in English discussions of the process. The goal of this approach is to ensure that children who are learning English as a second language have the opportunity to think about and discuss complex ideas in their native language. The approach is sometimes challenging, depending as it does on having a large enough number of fluent Spanish speakers in the group to make such conversations viable. The school's commitment to this bilingual approach requires continual support by parents, teachers, staff, and board members and affects the hiring process as well as the admission process. Despite the challenges, the school has maintained this program for several years.

Conclusions

Concepts Learned and Applications to Other Classrooms

Children in this preschool were clearly learning information about the life cycles of animals. Beyond learning facts, however, they were learning the process of doing science. Some important skills that were supported include: how to find out answers to their own questions, how to take multiple perspectives on the same phenomenon, and how to use books as resources. They were also learning that their own ideas are worth exploring in detail and sharing with other children and adults, and that these ideas can be changed and expanded through these interactions.

The teachers supported children's learning in many ways that could adapted to other classrooms. Giving students opportunities to choose a topic of study for the group can be challenging but the rewards come when the students show intense engagement in the topic. Other successful strategies used in this preschool include: spending some time at staff meetings reflecting on possible curriculum ideas based on what children are talking about; encouraging children to ask questions by working with small groups and trying to leave openings for children to initiate conversations; emphasizing the value of children's questions by writing them out on a large pad of paper or bulletin board; and referring back to interesting questions later in the day. Instead of always answering children's questions, teachers leave room for other children to discuss the answers and offer opinions. They model the process of discovery by looking for answers to questions in books or other sources, showing children that they don't have all the answers. They encourage the process of discovery by asking children for their predictions about what will happen and why.

Building bridges from home to school can also help to support children's learning. One strategy for doing this is to ask parents to keep track of children's questions and conversations at home about a particular topic being covered in school. This is a time-consuming task, however, and there are simpler ways to try and accomplish the same goals. For example, at each parent conference, teachers may check in with parents about children's particular interests and family experiences.

Preschoolers and Science

In this chapter, we have provided an illustration of how contextualized instruction looks in a particular series of projects in one preschool. We hope this example will be of interest for other preschool teachers who have similar goals for their classrooms. The example may also be of interest to teachers of older children, because it suggests that science instruction begins at a very early age and can build on the natural curiosity of young children.

As teachers and researchers we hope to have convinced readers that preschoolers can study biology. Of course, this is not meant as a suggestion to teach preschoolers science in a formal or academic way. In fact, academic skill-based instruction is not developmentally appropriate for young children (Elkind 1986; Hirsh-Pasek, Hyson, & Rescorla 1990). Instead, our view is that young children exhibit natural curiosity about the world (Gallas 1995) and that science instruction should perhaps capitalize more on this natural curiosity. Preschoolers ask "why" questions that rival those asked by philosophers and scientists (Callanan & Oakes 1992; Pérez-Granados & Callanan 1997), and their curiosity engages them with the world in sustained and thoughtful ways (Gallas 1995). As Lind (1997) argues, science is "a process of finding out and a system for organizing and reporting discoveries," and rather than a matter of memorizing of facts, "science is viewed as a way of thinking and working toward understanding the world" (75). With this definition, then, it seems uncontroversial to suggest that even preschoolers are constantly "doing science."

New directions in science teaching for older children are very consistent with the examples in this chapter (e.g., see Warren & Rosebery 1996). It is worth considering how children's preschool experiences may be linked more directly with later science education in the elementary grades. Vocabulary and mathematical concepts learned in the context of preschool activities could potentially provide a starting place for later, more advanced and systematic study. Children's curiosity in these early years seems already quite fully developed and perhaps even stronger than in older students. Finding ways to encourage this curiosity and build links to later school science seems an important goal for the future.

References

Bredekamp, S. 1987. *Developmentally Appropriate Practice in Early Childhood Programs Serving Children from Birth Through Age 8.* Washington, D.C.: National Association for the Education of Young Children.

Callanan, M. A., & L. M. Oakes. 1992. "Preschoolers' Questions and Parents' Explanations: Causal Thinking in Everyday Activity." *Cognitive Development* 7: 213–33.

Christian, D. 1996. "Two-Way Immersion Education: Students Learning Through Two Languages." *Modern Language Journal* 80: 66–76.

Derman-Sparks, L., & the ABC Task Force. 1989. *Anti-Bias Curriculum: Tools for Empowering Young Children.* Washington, D.C.: National Association for the Education of Young Children.

Elkind, D. 1986. "Formal Education and Early Childhood Education: An Essential Difference." *Phi Delta Kappan* 67: 631–36.

Gallas, K. 1995. *Talking Their Way into Science: Hearing Children's Questions and Theories, Responding with Curricula.* New York: Teachers College Press.

Hart, C., D. Burts, & R. Charlesworth. 1997. *Integrated Curriculum and Developmentally Appropriate Practice: Birth to Age Eight.* Albany: State University of New York Press.

Hirsh-Pasek, K., M. Hyson, & L. Rescorla. 1990. "Academic Environments in Preschool: Do They Pressure or Challenge Young Children?" *Early Education and Development* 1: 401–23.

Lind, K. K. 1997. "Science in the Developmentally Appropriate Integrated Curriculum." In *Integrated Curriculum and Developmentally Appropriate Practice: Birth to Age Eight,* ed. C. Hart, D. Burts, & R. Charlesworth, 75–101. Albany: State University of New York Press.

Lindholm, K. J. 1995. "Theoretical Assumptions and Empirical Evidence for Academic Achievement in Two Languages." In *Hispanic Psychology: Critical Issues in Theory and Research,* ed. A. Padilla, 273–87. Thousand Oaks, CA: Sage Publications.

Moll, L. C., & N. González. 1994. "Lessons from Research with Language Minority Children." *Journal of Reading Behavior* 26: 439–56.

Pérez-Granados, D. R., & M. A. Callanan. 1997. "Parents and Siblings as Early Resources for Young Children's Learning in Mexican-Descent Families." *Hispanic Journal of Behavioral Sciences* 19: 3–33.

Tharp, R. 1997. *From At-Risk to Excellence: Research, Theory, and Principles for Practice.* Santa Cruz, CA: Center for Research on Education, Diversity and Excellence.

Warren, B., & A. Rosebery. 1996. "'This Question Is Just Too, Too Easy!': Students' Perspectives on Accountability in Science." In *Innovations in Learning: New Environments for Education,* ed. L. Schauble & R. Glaser, 97–125. Mahwah, NJ: Erlbaum.

7

Agricultural Field Day

Linking Rural Cultures to School Lessons

ELLEN MCINTYRE, RUTH ANN SWEAZY & STACY GREER

It is a bright, clear day in mid-October in rural Kentucky. The sun is shining, but it is cold, and the brisk wind, crisp air, and soft reds and yellows of the oak and maple trees suggest impending winter. Crowds of Cane Creek Elementary[1] children are gathered in the school's adjacent ball field around various booths for demonstrations about agriculture and the environment. It's Cane Creek's annual Agricultural Field Day, planned by Ruth Ann and Stacy, two primary teachers. Tables are decorated for lunch with miniature haystacks, small painted gourds, and pumpkins. High school volunteers wearing their Future Farmers of

America jackets are about, assisting demonstrators, caring for animals, and serving food.

Ellen, Ruth Ann, and Stacy had been making family visits, modeled after the household visits described in Chapter Eleven of this volume, to the homes of their students in efforts to understand the children better, learn the cultural knowledge they hold, and better connect their home knowledge to what they do in school.[2] Through the visits, they learned that many families have extensive knowledge about agriculture and the environment. Specifically, they learned that all students had pets, including domestic farm animals, and the children were often expected to care for the animals. The children and their families were all familiar with farm equipment, safety rules, and general concepts about growing food. The teachers used this knowledge to make connections during their unit on agriculture and also built upon it to foster deeper understandings about economics, the environment, and the life cycle and to improve reading, writing, and mathematics skills.

Background

Cane Creek is a small town with a population of 800 within a county of 8,680. It is a rural area located about seventy-five minutes from a mid-size Kentucky city. The town has one small grocery store and three restaurants—a Dairy Queen, a cafeteria/gas station, and a small diner. Town residents live in old brick or frame homes or apartments, some government-subsidized, or in a trailer park on a hill in the center of town. Most schoolchildren and their families live in one of the many rural communities in the county surrounding the town, some of them in middle-class ranch-style homes, some on small farms, many in trailer parks or modest dwellings alongside country roads. In the last five years the county has experienced dramatic gentrification, as many people, tired of the city, have moved to "the country." The city newspaper has touted the county as having "land for cheap," and upper-middle-class people are buying land and building homes there (McIntyre & Stone 1998). While the county's population is changing, many Cane Creek Elementary students live at or near the poverty level and most can be characterized as poor black or white children of Appalachian descent.

Agricultural Field Day

As Stacy leads her class to some of the forty-five different stations, her primary grade children eagerly listen to and interact with the community volunteers. At one station, a young man named Charlie demonstrates how to use a power tool for germinating seeds. "What this machine does," he says as he kneels down and fingers the soil, "is it cuts a groove into the ground where the seeds can lie. Then, when it rains, it'll hold more water, and that helps the seeds germinate, or grow. It helps the seeds get down good into the soil." Then he asks the group, "Wanna see it?" and the children shout, "Yea!"

Charlie motions for the children to move back, turns on the loud machine, and the students watch as he rolls it across a smooth piece of earth. After a few minutes he turns off the tool, and the children hustle over to him to look at the ground. Charlie shows them the new grooves and says, "Now, I can do about eight pounds per square foot, but I have to do an acre, and that takes a whole lot of work."

Later, after a demonstration of how corn gets from the husk to the microwave popcorn bag and one about how milk gets from the cow to the carton, the children find themselves talking with Betty Lou, a member of the Kentucky Gourd Society. Gourds are common artifacts in Cane Creek, but Betty Lou expands the children's knowledge of their uses. She holds up a skinny, four-foot-long gourd and compares it to gourds in Africa. "This one is the longest I've got, but in Africa, there are gourds so big that people carve boats out of them! Some even use them for huts! They are called Nigerian Giants." She goes on, explaining the uses of gourds in Kentucky and elsewhere. "Many people make music with gourds—some are drums . . . " and she beats on one shaped like a drum, " . . . and some are made into rattles," and she shakes a rattle gourd. She then picks up a small one, shaped like a turtle, and plays a tune. "This one is called an African gourd thumb piano." She shows the children other gourds of all shapes and sizes, many painted with exotic designs and bold colors. She says, "You can do anything with a gourd that your imagination will let you do!" Betty Lou ends the demonstration with directions on how the children can grow and harvest their own gourds.

Later, after viewing the many animal exhibits—cows, horses, pigs, goats, chickens, turkeys, rabbits, a rooster, and a swan—the children admire the many shiny tractors and their corresponding trophies won in tractor pull competitions. Stacy urges the children forward, eager for them to witness the demonstration of safe uses of familiar household and farm items.

Wayne, owner of a fertilizer company, holds up a bottle of liquid soap and reminds the children to be very careful to always read the label before using a product. He explains that "this soap is for cleaning equipment, not for your hands or arms; it could burn you." He describes what to do with old motor oil cans and spray paint cans. He demonstrates proper disposal of chemicals and warns, "they must be kept in a locked place at all times." Then he shows the children how to use the fire extinguisher, again reminding them that they must have an adult around to practice.

Later that day, one of the children, Rusty, asks a farmer, "How sharp is that blade?" as he points to the bottom of a combine. "Real sharp," James Martin replies. "It'll cut you in two." James and his twelve-year-old son have just finished a demonstration of how corn goes from the stalk in the field to the grain in a bag in a grocery store. They have three pieces of equipment with them—a combine, a tractor, and an eighteen-wheel truck—and they use the vehicles to explain the process, emphasizing safety the entire time. The children listen intently, especially as the boy talks, and are filled with questions after the demonstration. "How much does a combine cost?" (A lot.) "How many acres do you do a day?" (Forty to fifty.), "How much corn do you get in one day?" (Four thousand bushels, depending on conditions and timing.)

The rest of the day is spent listening to and watching demonstrations and explanations of the water cycle, electrical power and safety, how much grain it takes to feed cattle, and more. The children eat ice cream and talk and play and eventually wearily sit on the grass to rest. They've learned a lot because they have been able to link their previous classroom lessons to what they have seen and heard on this field day. They will learn a lot more, too, as the teachers continue to make further connections to classroom work in the days to come.

Links Between Community and Classroom

In the days preceding Agricultural Field Day, Ruth Ann and Stacy prepared their primary grade children (kindergarten through grade 3) for what they might learn. They wanted to capitalize on children's rural backgrounds and knowledge of farming to help them learn deeper concepts about agriculture and the environment and to improve their reading, writing, and problem-solving skills and strategies through work the children would find meaningful.

They began by reading aloud many books about farming, including an "Eyewitness" book, *Farm* (Halley 1996); *Mighty Machines: Tractors and Other Farm Machines* (Kindersley 1995), which was very popular with the boys; *All About Seeds* (Berger 1992); many titles on farm animals; and many emergent and beginning reader trade books, including *Thanks to Cows* (Fowler 1992) and a "Rookie Read-Aloud" book from the science series that explains the milking process. The teachers encouraged the children to read these books during independent reading time (many were at the appropriate developmental level), and they discussed them with the children in efforts to create instructional conversations (Tharp & Gallimore 1993), which are discussions that help students develop concepts—talk that teaches.

During the weeks prior to the field day, children were observed sorting and classifying seeds and learning the conditions needed for seeds to grow. They grew their own plants and predicted growth of various seeds, and they identified, wrote about, and drew various parts of plants. They learned about the life cycle of plants and later connected that to the life cycle of animals.

Mathematics concepts and skills played a large part as the teachers had students measure milk, measure by "horse hands," graph farm foods they like to eat, estimate how much popcorn can be popped from one cup of kernels, and estimate how much can be planted on an acre. These skills culminated in a lesson on farm economics—how much money it takes to run a farm. Art activities included basket weaving (Ruth Ann and Stacy are experts), designing quilts, and painting gourds.

A few lessons that focused on animals are described later. These were adapted from a unit designed by the Kentucky State Farm Bureau Federation (Lowe 1992) and are among the activities Ruth Ann and Stacy choose from each year.

Ruth Ann and Stacy began with a familiar lesson, "Animals on the Farm." Some of the objectives included (1) describing characteristics of several farm animals, (2) describing ways farmers care for the animals, (3) listing foods derived from farm animals, and (4) using oral and written language to learn these concepts and skills. Beginning with what students already knew, the class made a table, much like a K–W–L chart (Ogle 1990), that included the information above. Thus they began with students' home and cultural knowledge. Then to expand on this knowledge, the teachers read aloud several books, including *Farm Animals* (Children's Nature Library 1991); *Pigs* (Munsch 1989), a funny story with many facts about pigs; *Good Morning, Chick* (Ginsburg & Barton 1980), a similar book; and *Inside a Barn in the Country* (Capucilli & Arnold 1995), a rebus read-along story. The teachers and children kept a chart of all new information learned from these books.

To ensure that texts and tasks were developmentally appropriate for the their students, the teachers were careful to balance fiction and nonfiction, and they balanced read-alouds with books the children read by themselves. For example, they used "Sunshine Books" (Wright Group 1988), which have very predictable texts, for their emergent readers and magazines and encyclopedias that the teachers read to the children. They showed pictures of farm animals and real photos from farms in the community and continued to work on developing instructional conversations. One child, Jason, the son of tenant farmers, was able to explain to the other children that cows have to be milked twice a day and that they use machines, not hands, to do the milking on farms. During one week, the older children selected an animal to research, using the many books the teachers collected for the unit, and they added new details to the table.

A second set of lessons was called "Milk—From the Cow to Me!" The goals included (1) describing the process by which cows convert feed and water to milk and how farms get the milk to the consumer, (2) using food paths to trace other common products from the farm to the consumer, and (3) developing students' oral, written, and mathematics skills as they learned the concepts. By understanding how milk gets from the cow to the table, children are helped to understand other similar change processes in their lives. Two good books they used for this lesson were *Thanks to Cows* (Fowler 1992) and *Milk: From Cow to Carton* (Aliki 1992).

One day, the teachers filled a plastic swimming pool with twenty-nine gallons of water, filled a box with twenty pounds of grain, and brought in seventy-five pounds of hay (about two bales). After observing and discussing this scene, the teachers told the children that this is what one cow consumes in a day! Then, they asked questions such as "What would the room look like if we had feed for two cows? Three cows? Four? How many rooms of feed would we need to store enough food and water for twenty cows?" [3] These conceptual economics and mathematics problems were discussed and wondered about, and children had the opportunity to draw or write about their thinking. Ruth Ann and Stacy explained, "These estimation skills are not only important for young children in school, but they are skills farmers use every day."

After Agricultural Field Day, Ruth Ann and Stacy helped students make sense of what they saw and heard through much discussion and writing activities. They continued to read books on agriculture and implemented a recycling program in their rooms. The children quite naturally read books they were familiar with and wrote in their journals in response to field day. One student wrote an unsolicited letter to Ruth Ann (Figure 7–1).

When asked about student learning from this unit, Ruth Ann said:

> They love this time of year, especially the olders [children who have returned to their classroom for a second or third year]. It seems like kids learn more when they think they already know about a topic, I guess because they are excited, like, "Oh yeah, we did this last year" . . . but their products are better and they learn a little more each time.

When asked about using families as resources for teaching, Stacy said:

> The parents have so much information that I would never have known—what the child likes, hobbies, how the child deals with stress. They've spent six years with the child, or seven, or eight. And they have that much expertise which I am trying to catch up.

Dear Ms. Sweazy,

I Like Ag Day a lot.
I think it very Edicational
in many was such As.
it tells you about Farm and
home Safety, And how milk
is good For You, and how
many things you can Do
with a gourd, And Lot more
Edicational uses.
I think we Should
Countinue Doing Ag Day
every year because its
Edicational and most
People enjoy it. I
know I Do.

Sincedy,
Courtney stump

Figure 7–1.

Strategies for Connecting Home and School

All of these lessons are examples of how Ruth Ann and Stacy connect school learning to their Agricultural Field Day. They use techniques described in Chapter One for connecting their students' cultural knowledge to the school curriculum and expanding it, much like the teachers of Latino students described in Chapters Three and Nine. For example, the teachers designed instructional activities based on what students already knew from home, community, and school. Since these children lived in a rural community, many were familiar with farming. Some lived on farms, and all had at least visited farms. Using this knowledge as a basis for more knowledge is not only respectful of their cultural funds of knowledge (González et al. 1995) but also based on how young children learn—through building on what they already know.

These teachers assisted students in connecting and applying their knowledge to issues in the home and community. During these lessons, Ruth Ann and Stacy encouraged the children to take what they had learned and practice it at home—everything from planting gourd seeds and watching them grow to safety practices with household items and recycling. In these ways, they made the classroom lessons truly authentic.

Finally, these teachers provided opportunities for parents and community members to participate in classroom instructional activities. Ruth Ann and Stacy began early, asking for volunteers to help with the field day. They were in contact year-round with the community members who shared their expertise and the parents who agreed to assist the teachers during this day. All involved seemed to feel a sense of community and cohesiveness. It enabled the teachers to have good relations with the parents and community for the rest of the school year. Parents commented on how impressed they were with what the teachers did for the children. Many requested that their younger children get placed in their classrooms in subsequent years. For children of poverty, having a regular, positive school connection is rare, but these teachers see to it that this happens for all their students.

Notes

1. All names except for Ellen, Ruth Ann, and Stacy are pseudonyms.

2. The work the teachers are doing, such as family visits, is part of their participation in a research project funded by the Center for Research on Education, Diversity, and Excellence (CREDE), as are all the studies portrayed in this book. In this project, instruction and Agricultural Field Day were documented through field notes, interviews, and video- and audiotapes. Family information was collected through field notes and interviews.

3. Some of the lessons are recollections of Ruth Ann and Stacy's teaching and were not taken from the data set.

References

Aliki. 1992. *Milk: From Cow to Carton.* New York: HarperCollins.

Berger, M. 1992. *All About Seeds.* New York: Scholastic.

Capucilli, S., & T. Arnold. 1995. *Inside a Barn in the Country.* New York: Scholastic.

Children's Nature Library. 1991. *Farm Animals.* Lincolnwood, IL: Gallery Books.

Fowler, A. 1992. *Thanks to Cows.* Chicago: Children's Press.

Ginsburg, M., & B. Barton. 1980. *Good Morning, Chick.* New York: Scholastic.

González, N., L. Moll, M. Tenery, A. Rivera, P. Rendon, R. González, & C. Amanti. 1995. "Funds of Knowledge for Teaching in Latino Households." *Urban Education* 29 (4): 443–71.

Halley, N. 1996. *Farm.* New York: Alfred A. Knopf.

Kindersley, D. 1995. *Mighty Machines: Tractors and Other Farm Machines.* New York: Dorling Kindersley.

Lowe, S. 1992. *Kentucky Curriculum Framework: Course of Study.* Frankfort, KY: Kentucky Department of Education.

McIntyre, E., & N. Stone. 1998. "Culturally Contextualized Instruction in Appalachian Descent and African American Classrooms." In *47th Yearbook of the National Reading Conferences,* ed. T. Shanahan and F. V. Rodriguez-Brown. Chicago: National Reading Conference.

Moll, L. C., C. Amanti, D. Neff, & N. González. 1992. "Funds of Knowledge for Teaching: Using a Qualitative Approach to Connect Home and Classrooms." *Theory Into Practice* 31: 131–41.

Munsch, R. 1989. *Pigs.* Toronto: Annick Press.

Ogle, D. 1990. "K–W–L: The Know, Want to Know, Learn Strategy." In *Children's Comprehension of Text,* ed. K. D. Muth, 205–23. Newark, DE: International Reading Association.

Tharp, R., & R. Gallimore. 1993. *Rousing Minds to Life: Teaching, Learning, and Schooling in Social Context.* New York: Cambridge University Press.

8

Teaching History

A Cultural Approach for Primary Grade Children

ELLEN MCINTYRE WITH JOANN ARCHIE

One of the common attributes of successful teachers of African American children is that they express cultural solidarity with their students (Foster 1997) or connect in some way to their lives (Ladson-Billings 1994). In JoAnn's primary classroom (grades 1, 2, and 3), cultural solidarity is a hallmark of her instruction. The focus of her interactions is on community building, and all instruction extends from that philosophy. Her teaching is based on the assumption that all children can learn, in fact, that all students in her classroom *will* learn at high levels. JoAnn connects with her black and white students through a deep understanding of the students'

language patterns, interaction styles, current cultural norms, and historical traditions.

Background

JoAnn was raised and currently resides in the urban, mostly African American neighborhood in which she teaches. The neighborhood is noted for high poverty and high crime but also for housing many successful black businesses, beautiful parks, and a residential section known for its stately homes along tree-lined boulevards.

JoAnn teaches at Rudolph Elementary,[1] a large urban school located in her neighborhood, which is adjacent to the downtown area. The school sits among dilapidated buildings as well as modern facilities. It resides in the middle of an acre with huge oak trees and a new playground, formerly the site of a veterans hospital. The building is new, with a large, spacious corridor decorated with traditional and modern art. Nearly all the children in the school qualify for the federal free breakfast and lunch programs and more than half live in one-parent homes. The principal is an energetic African American woman whose goal is to increase the achievement of all students. She recently sponsored an overnight event for children for community building and then gave the participating teachers the following afternoon off to "recover."

Because she lives in the community in which she teaches, JoAnn has an understanding of the cultural norms, routines, participation structures, and interaction patterns common for this population, though she is keenly aware of differences between individuals. She can visit with her students' families at the grocery store, church, or local restaurants. She is aware of some of the funds of knowledge the families hold because she knows many of them on a personal basis. For a long time, JoAnn has had a mission to teach in culturally appropriate and responsible ways. Throughout her adulthood, she has been conscious of injustices of the educational system, particularly the cultural mismatch between European American teachers and school administrators and African American children. She remembers her own miscommunications with her teachers as a child because her language was different from theirs and because much of the curriculum seemed foreign to her. She is well aware of the communication patterns and participation structures of the children in her classroom because these children—both black and white—live in the community in which she was born and raised and still lives. Her background provides the foundation for the community-building focus she maintains in her classroom.

Community is achieved in part through extensive honest discussion with her students.[2] JoAnn openly addresses differences between herself and her students, including race as a natural point of reference. Under the broad theme of change, JoAnn began the school year focusing on relationships in the classroom, school, home, and community. She explicitly teaches children how to treat one another, and her classroom is filled with bulletin boards reflecting her philosophy. JoAnn strives to teach responsibility, inviting the children to create the class rules and teaching them to monitor their own adherence to the rules. While she offers much student choice in learning activity, JoAnn communicates her expectations that students choose wisely, for they must complete the work they begin. Aware of the local norms and expectations for student achievement, she varies her activities to reflect student preferences and developmental levels. She also uses an abundance of literature for, about, and by African Americans to teach reading, writing, mathematics, history, and science and makes conscience efforts to link the language and content of the books to the children's experiences.

History with a Cultural Focus

For many of us, the teaching of American history has traditionally had a European focus. Through history books, students first study Columbus. They are introduced to Native Americans through the perspective of Europeans who had come to explore, conquer, and settle the new world.

JoAnn has a multiple-perspectives approach to teaching. That is, she tries to get her students to look at events from all sides. JoAnn began with the study of regions of the country. After connecting places the children had heard or read about to their home city and state and conducting some lessons on map-reading skills, she introduced a study of Native Americans in the Southwest, explaining that particular nations usually ended up in the same geographic area in the United States.

"The Timucua nation is located in the Southwest," she said, pointing to the map.

A child asked her to repeat the name, and she did. A few children giggled. JoAnn gently replied, "Remember that some people laugh at African names? We need to remember that when we hear Indian names." She read books to the children about the nation, eliciting from them how this tribe lives differently than they do. Afterward, JoAnn directed children to read a section of a textbook that relates to Southeast Indian culture from the pre-Colonial period. Then she led them in a discussion about the concept of culture:

"Tell me something you learned from the reading. What is culture?"

"Clothes . . . [unintelligible] the clothes and the food," one child said.

"What about the clothes and food?"

"Religion!" another child piped up.

"What about religion?"

"People have different religions."

"Yes, we do. The Timucua all believed in the same God, the same beliefs. Here in Louisville, there might be one kind of church on one corner, then on the next street you might have a different kind of church; we have many different religions. Religion is just part of culture. You were right, clothes and food are another part. Culture is a way a group of people live. People can be living in the same neighborhood, but live differently."

"Like we wear clothes."

"Well, it is more than that. It's not just wearing clothes, it is the kind you wear. When I went to the Bahamas, I noticed the way they dressed. I never wear clothes with no sleeves or shorts. That's part of my culture—what I believe. When I was in the Bahamas, I saw that everyone wore clothes with no sleeves, and I was very hot, so that showed me that they wear clothes like that because of the heat, and that is part of their culture."

Some of the children began discussing their clothes. JoAnn reminded them that culture is more than clothes. "It is the food you eat, the way you talk, the games you play, religion, the work people do—like many Indians were farmers—all about how you live." And later, "Now, go back to your books. Read it again, and think about the culture of the Timucua. Then take a few minutes to write about what you read."

Later in the week, the students read about Navajo, Anasasi, Zuni, and Hopi nations. During the course of the unit, the students made maps, read many books, and wrote essays on what they had learned. Through these lessons, students examined each tribe's culture and compared the information to cultures of today such as Navajo, Anasasi, Indian, and others. She emphasized similarities as well as differences, always encouraging critical thinking.

JoAnn invited the students to write their answers to the following questions: "What would have been good about living in the past as a Native American in the Southwest? What would have been bad about this? What would have been interesting?" During writing time, JoAnn played desert and Native American flute music. Writing sessions were often followed by sharing and grand instructional conversations (Tharp & Gallimore 1993) led by JoAnn. In these conversations, children had opportunities to expand on concepts they learned.

On another day the children formed small groups and made pueblos out of cardboard boxes covered with a flour mixture that they painted on with brushes. This was in preparation for a large display of a reservation they later used for a class performance. On other days, the students learned to weave, make sand paintings (they spread glue on paper, covered it with sand, then made designs in the sand), and make turquoise jewelry. On each occasion,

JoAnn asked the students how they thought they could go about getting their materials and working together productively. She later asked them where they would like to store their products. In these ways, she combines classroom content with her community-building philosophy.

After spending considerable time on the Southwest, JoAnn moved on to studying the Plains nations, Southeastern nations, and lastly the Woodlands nations at the time of Thanksgiving, when she finally introduced the history of the Pilgrims.

One day JoAnn gave each child a little teacher-made booklet for them to read and illustrate. A section of the text read, "Native Americans lived in this land. Explorers arrived and thought it was grand. The pilgrims landed and stayed here. Indians helped them survive that first year." The children read and illustrated their books and participated in classroom discussions about what it might have been like for the Native Americans when the Europeans came to their country.

"What do you think? Were they glad they [the Pilgrims] came?" JoAnn asked one day.

None of the children responded, so she went on, "You have to think; the natives were used to doing things their way. They used the land the way they wanted. They planted their corn. . . . Yes, the Pilgrims also wanted to plant corn, but they also came and decided that certain sections of land were theirs. They started farms, sometimes on land that the natives had been using." The discussion ensued, and JoAnn attempted to help children understand both the advantages and disadvantages to having the early settlers come to America. Her goal was to help children see history through the eyes of all the participants.

Later in the school year, when focusing on the westward movement, JoAnn used the book *Wagon Wheels* (Brenner 1993), which is about a black family moving west, and later they read *The Josefina Story Quilt,* on the same topic. The class participated in simulations, discussions, and eventually a play about the westward movement.

One day, JoAnn was observed saying to the children, "You pretend it is the 1800s and you are moving west. You have a long adventure ahead of you. You have to go over the Rocky Mountains . . . and you're going in a wagon train. Here are some things you could take." She pointed to a list of items on a chart and continued, "A grandfather clock, medicine, farming tools, chains to pull you over the mountain, a hatchet, food, a rocking chair, and a rifle."

A child asked, "If we are going through the Rocky Mountains, will we see animals?"

JoAnn nodded and told them, "You have to decide what to pack. If you pack too much, you won't be able to move the wagons." She explained that they were to rank-order the items, complimenting one child as he began by saying, "I see Mike crossing off each item as he puts it on his new list; if you do that, it will keep you organized." She then asked them to each write an essay explaining why they put the first three items at the top of the list and why they put their last three at the bottom.

Janine came up to JoAnn, eager to share her work. She read her list and explanation: "I would take food, water, and chains. Food you have to eat and water you have to drink." JoAnn asked her, "Is there another way to get water?" The child said, "The river?" And JoAnn responded, "You have to think about everything, carefully." Winnie said, "Food and medicine, because if someone got sick and they didn't have medicine they would have to go back home and get some more."

While working through this yearlong unit on American history, the students made booklets with poems about each different historical period. The booklets consisted of four pages, one each for Native Americans, Pilgrims, and the first Thanksgiving; the Revolutionary War; slavery and the Civil War; and the westward movement. Each page was divided into four sections with a poem for each topic. The children drew pictures in each section illustrating the poem. On their own, the children started reading the poems together, turning them into raps, an activity JoAnn encouraged. They put themselves into groups, practiced, and performed the raps for the class.

Connections Between Curriculum and Community

Throughout the teaching of American history during this school year, JoAnn helped children see multiple perspectives, enabling them to become critical thinkers. She avoided the traditional Eurocentric model of teaching American history and focused instead on helping students understand how events might have been perceived by nondominant groups such as Native Americans and African Americans.

A multiple-perspectives approach infuses JoAnn's curriculum. She spends a lot of time just talking with the children as preparation for writing or during their morning meeting time, which is designated for discussion of what the day will hold or other issues both inside and outside the classroom that need to be addressed. During these meetings, which often become problem-solving sessions, she does little of the actual talking. Students do the thinking in the classroom; in fact, she has a big sign in her room above her desk as a reminder: "Who is doing the thinking in this classroom?" She assists her students in applying what they know to some of the issues that exist in the classroom, their homes, and the community. Some of the topics have centered around how to keep the learning centers clean and organized, taking turns, and how to show respect for one another during writing workshop sharing time. One child said, "You have to listen to each other and ask questions about what they write." Issues about home and community have included recycling, child care, cooking meals for the family, littering, and neighborhood safety. When a child speaks about not being able to sleep at night out of fear, JoAnn understands on a level most teachers cannot because she, too, hears the gunshots. JoAnn addresses these topics, rather than avoiding them, whenever they come up. She also regularly incorporates student reflection in her lessons, asking the children to think about what they have learned. In these ways, she connects to students' home cultures by showing respect for who they are and modeling respect for others as well.

Notes

1. All names, except for JoAnn's, are pseudonyms.

2. JoAnn was part of a CREDE study. The teaching described here was collected through field notes and videotape.

References

Brenner, B. 1993. *Wagon Wheels.* New York: Harper & Row.

Coerr, E. 1999. *The Josefina Story Quilt.* Burnsville, MN: Econo-Clad Books.

Foster, M. 1997. *Black Teachers on Teaching.* New York: New Press.

Greenfield, E. 1994. *Nathanial Talking.* New York: Children's Press.

Ladson-Billings, G. 1994. *The Dreamkeepers: Successful Teachers of African American Children.* San Francisco: Jossey-Bass.

Tharp, R., & R. Gallimore. 1993. *Rousing Minds to Life: Teaching, Learning, and Schooling in Social Context.* New York: Cambridge University Press.

9

Creating Learning Communities

The "Build Your Dream House" Unit

MELANIE AYERS, JOSÉ DAVID FONSECA,
ROSI ANDRADE & MARTA CIVIL

Our ongoing work with teacher-researcher study groups in the BRIDGE project has laid the foundation for helping teachers develop skills to research student households for their mathematical potential and subsequent use in the classroom. In the following narrative, teacher-researcher José David Fonseca shares his experiences in creating a curriculum unit for very specific needs, with an initially aggressive group of disenfranchised middle school students. As a teacher he was concerned with the motivation of students in the engagement of meaningful learning activity, aligned to students' real-life, lived experiences, while at the same time focusing on the demands of the mathematics curriculum at their respective levels. This work explores the implications of the rationale guiding our project, which views learning as an interactive process while seeking to define what mathematics can be within the tension between its practical applications, curricular definitions, and the beliefs and values held by teacher-researchers like José David Fonseca, parents, and students. This narrative respects teacher-researchers' thoughts on the process and is reflective of how the ethnographic experience provided that initial lens for looking into community stores of knowledge. Although we are not looking at all households and are not tied to a particular fund of knowledge, we rely on ethnography as a tool, with each household visit adding to our accumulating store of perceptions of funds of knowledge. A discussion at the end of this chapter will focus on making connections between researchers' respective work and the current state of mathematics.

José David Fonseca

At the time of this work I was a seventh- and eighth-grade mathematics instructor at a middle school in southern Tucson, Arizona, within the same school district as Leslie Kahn (Chapter Four) and Caroline Carson (Chapter Ten). The local Mexican working-class community surrounding the school is replete with cultural traditions and practices amidst families in their daily struggle to meet the challenges and demands of raising their children. The middle school is characterized as 95 percent Hispanic. As for me, I accepted the position as a bilingual mathematics instructor at the middle school shortly after earning a master's degree in bilingual education with a mathematics specialty at the University of Arizona. However, I already held an undergraduate degree in civil engineering from a university in Mexico and had completed graduate coursework toward a master's program in mathematics where I also taught university courses in mathematics, some for architects. I also have experience in construction and as a construction site manager. Unbeknownst to me at the time, it would be these earlier experiences in conjunction with my funds of knowledge experience that would more readily support my new teaching assignment at this middle school, as I shall explain.

I was very excited about the teaching position and even more pleased that the middle school had adopted a strong mathematics core curriculum. Once in the classroom, I soon found myself disappointed to see that the curriculum did not meet the real needs of my students as learners. I realized that the students needed a strong mathematics curriculum that would build on their prior experiences and understanding of mathematics. Also, whereas my own educational background prepared me well for the theoretical preparations of being a mathematics teacher, my idealistic notions based on formal educational training did not prepare me for the real experiences of teaching mathematics in this unfamiliar inner-city context. The students that I had taught in Mexico were university age, they were motivated to learn, and they had been educated in a system in which teachers were much more respected. My middle school experience, also with students of Mexican origin, challenged those very perspectives that I held about students' views of teaching and learning.

At the beginning of the school year, I suspected there were two main reasons that the learning activities based on the curriculum were not working. First, the students demonstrated negative attitudes about school and displayed disruptive behavior in the classroom. I also noticed a lack of motivation on the part of the students to attend class, complete class assignments, and work on supplemental activities. More telling, however, was the mathematics diagnostic test on the use of basic operations that I administered to my seventh- and eighth-grade students. Their scores showed that the average was at a third- to fourth-grade mathematics level. I quickly realized that the only way to solve these two issues was to address the more immediate academic needs of the students and find a way to motivate them.

Funds of Knowledge Survey

In light of this pressing situation, I moved to implement an ethnographic study, which included household visits. I was guided to do so through the field experience graduate course on funds of knowledge that I was taking at the time, offered through the College of Education by Professors Luis Moll and Norma González. This became the precursor to my involvement in the BRIDGE project. I also formulated and administered a survey to students in all of my classes (five classes of approximately twenty-eight students each). From this, a wealth of information about my students and their families was uncovered, which I later used to create a mathematics project to help resolve the complexities of the classroom. Of those students who responded, I found that 99 percent represented a working-class, Hispanic population. Construction made up 60 percent of the occupations of my students' parents. The survey also revealed that the other 40 percent of working parents were employed as automobile mechanics, plumbers, seamstresses, and so on.

Another finding suggested that the students' homes were small and crowded; many students were living with just one parent, primarily mothers;

and many other social constraints complicated other families' living arrangements. I reflected on these ethnographic findings and when I looked more closely at them, I began to think about what kind of project would be useful to motivate these students. I felt that if I could motivate and positively influence students' attitudes, then it might be possible to get them to work differently in class. The "Build Your Dream House" project that began to develop in my head seemed the perfect vehicle for motivating students to learn mathematics while elevating their mathematical performance levels.

The "Build Your Dream House" Project

One of the early in-class brainstorming sessions with the students reaffirmed the significance of students' desires to live in larger, nicer houses, with their own bedrooms and accessories. For example, when I asked one young man to describe his house, he said he lived with his seven brothers—and, of course, his parents—in a small house with only two bedrooms and one bathroom. The idea of eight individuals sharing a small two-bedroom house puzzled me, so I asked where he slept. He replied that he slept with two of his brothers on a small bed, while the other brothers slept in the living room and kitchen areas. Further, when relatives came to visit the family, even more people utilized the same limited space. Accommodating large families and extended family visits in small dwellings is commonplace for working-class families, who do not have the economic means to afford middle- and upper-class luxuries. Knowing that these living quarters must be difficult, I next asked the student, "If you could redesign your house, would you? What would you do?" The young man replied, "Oh, yes, I would like to have a bedroom for myself, a swimming pool, and a four-car garage." The appeal of the project was that it was a dream not uncommon to any one of my students.

Through the project I also sought to motivate students to learn mathematics by building on their background knowledge and prior experiences as suggested by the survey responses. Knowing from the surveys that the majority of my students had some knowledge of construction activities through experiences with their parents, grandparents, and extended family, I relied on my own knowledge of architecture and construction as a basis to create a series of learning activities for them. I feel that it is important to begin from the actual situation, but always with an eye for the real academic potential of the student. If students begin at another level, then it becomes difficult for them to reach this higher level by themselves. You need to take small steps before making giant leaps. Thus, I used the information gathered through the interviews and diagnostic tests to begin teaching mathematical concepts, building on the mathematics that the students already understood.

Although student motivation was just the first obstacle to overcome, the core curriculum was always at the center of the long-term project I had set before us. Connecting the construction project to the entire core curriculum, which includes geometry, probability, fractions, algebra, and problem solving, was a challenge. At first, the connection was not clear. After some thought, I decided to divide the construction project into several smaller parts: constructing the dream house (scale drawings, 3-D visualization, measurement); abstracting the geometry used in designing a house (algebra, geometry, 3-D visualization); and estimating costs and calculating various materials needed (fractions, probability, problem solving). These then fell into the various phases of the curriculum unit.

Project Phases

The first stage of the long-term project began when I asked students to draw two-dimensional floor plans of their dream houses using only paper and pencil. The designs, of course, were rough sketches. After the students had completed their drawings, I showed them a blueprint of a real floor plan, using the correct architectural symbols for doors, windows, toilets, sinks, and so on. I asked them if they also wanted to learn how to employ the tools of professional architects, such as rulers, triangles, T-squares, levelers, and computer software. The response was unanimous; they wanted to learn how to use these tools so that they could professionally design their own dream houses. At this point, students' interest in the project peaked. In the first part of the yearlong project, the students developed the skills of measurement, proportion, and scaling through an intense emphasis on drawing. They also learned basic operations such as computing area and perimeter and were shown the strategies that real construction workers use in building, such as "tracing" two walls, a process of joining two walls at right angles.

Once these activities were completed, the second part of the project began. Here the focus shifted from the experience of designing a dream house to conceptualizing and abstracting geometrical concepts. The focus became shapes, not the house. I used this opportunity to abstract the mathematics embedded in the construction project, by encouraging highly sophisticated discussions on geometry. For example, the students developed generalizable formulas to calculate the areas, perimeters, and angles of sections of regular polygons. They also developed a general equation to calculate the scaling factor for any floor plan. These discussions of ratio, fractions, and proportion connected the construction project and the mathematical concepts of the core curriculum.

After the students learned how to draw floor plans and analyze the geometric properties of a house, the next process was to get the students to solve problems related to building a new house structure. The students determined the amount of material needed to construct their dream homes, found measurements of their designs, decided how many light fixtures they needed for all of the rooms, and calculated the number of tiles and amount of carpet needed to cover the walls and floors. For this part of the project students needed to estimate the cost per square unit or per cubic unit, depending on the type of materials utilized (e.g., tile, carpet, cement, or roofing). Students attempted to minimize costs by manipulating the perimeters and areas of their designs, thus suggesting the authenticity of the project activity.

Additionally, I used actual data from a local real estate company to introduce the core curriculum topics of probability and statistics. For example, I had students compute the average price of homes in Tucson. Depending on the floor plan (e.g., two-bedroom, two-bathroom, two-story, etc.) of each dream house, I also had the students compute the average price of a similar structure from the section of town they wanted to live in. The students learned to construct histograms and how to connect the points to find the mean. Each student also investigated the probability that the price of his or her dream house was within a certain price range, based on the local real estate data. Thus, the use of actual data in the context of real situations was ripe for the discussion of probability and statistics.

The project culminated with each team of students presenting their construction projects in front of other class members, the principal, parents, and community members. Students eloquently described their designs, provided reasons for each particular design, stated the mathematical formulas that they used for their construction, and concisely summarized the total costs for using their construction strategies. All of us present were impressed with the final products, especially because they were reflective of the difficulty of the work and the investments made by students. In thinking about the entire process and the investment made by the students during the course of it, I was reminded of an earlier incident with one male student in particular. When I originally told him that his house would be very expensive and asked how he was going to get the money to build it, I recall that he flippantly replied that he would sell drugs. At the end of the year, however, when I asked him what his proyecto de vida (life project) would be, he said he wanted to be an architect. On a personal note, it was encouraging to see such transformations. Many such students who entered the school year with a negative attitude toward learning and teaching that contributed to their own reluctance to learn mathematics left the class with a newfound confidence in their mathematics abilities and pleasantly surprised with their experience and own talents.

Reflections

I now realize, as I had suggested at the beginning, that there were two additional factors that contributed to the success of this long-term construction unit, aside from the more important decision to begin with students' knowledge and experiences. They are attributable to my own funds of knowledge, that is, experiences with architecture, drafting, and construction, my mathematical background, and especially my affinity for geometry. I feel that geometry is an essential mathematical subject for understanding our surroundings. Geometry is everywhere. It is in everything—our bodies, motion, and so on. Thus, choosing a curriculum unit in which geometry served as a basis for teaching mathematical concepts seemed appropriate. Additionally, my familiarity with the tools and strategies that architects, draftsmen, and construction workers use on the job and my interests in geometry and architecture combined to make the curriculum unit long-lasting and enjoyable for students and me. I feel that my own pedagogical beliefs about teaching mathematics also played a significant role in the success of the "Build Your Dream House" project. I strongly feel that students should create their own mathematics. For me, the teacher has three important roles: advisor, question poser, and problem poser. I used these three roles to engage students in their own construction of mathematics.

Discussion and Implications of the Work

José David's narrative, like Leslie Kahn's narrative in Chapter Four, reflects a shared common goal of developing curriculum theme units that offer the potential for building on their respective students' knowledge, experiences, and interests while at the same time helping those students advance in their learning of academic mathematics. The narratives also attest to the level of commitment that this kind of work entails, not only on the part of the teacher but on the part of students as well. Both projects were long-term, yet students persisted and were engaged throughout. Also, not lost on anyone reading their narratives is that both Leslie and José David spent a great deal of out-of-school time accessing and gathering necessary resources, developing activities, and constantly reflecting on and revising their plans as needed, all without losing sight of an overarching framework. While both were knowledgeable in the themes explored (architecture in Jose David's case; gardening in Leslie's), recall that these themes were also part of the funds of knowledge of many of their students and their families. As teachers, Leslie and José David shared a willingness to actively listen to their students' voices, and in turn, find out about their needs and their desires as learners. These narratives shed some light on questions that we have been pondering here and elsewhere: What might a learning environment look like if we tried to develop more participation-oriented approaches toward the learning of mathematics (similar to what these and other students experience in their out-of-school lives)? What might be the implications for the mathematical education of students if we took their lived experiences and backgrounds as resources for learning in the classroom? As an aside, Leslie's own motivation for being in project BRIDGE, for example, was to explore whether "rigorous" mathematics (study of perimeter and area) could be developed from everyday mathematics (chicken wire dilemma).

In José David's "Build Your Dream House" project, he and the students had to balance the appeal of focusing on the aesthetic characteristics (making the models look good) with a more serious exploration of the mathematics in the creation of the models. As a teacher, José David had to bridge from the practical context of house building to the more formal abstraction of mathematics. But, perhaps more insightfully, he had to develop mathematically rich activities that would allow students to see how knowing more mathematics could help them make better models. Knowing mathematics is then seen as a resource toward their goal.

10

Creating Links Between Home and School Mathematics Practices

NORMA GONZÁLEZ, ROSI ANDRADE & CAROLINE CARSON

This chapter focuses on the knowledge and experience that children and their families have and the potential for that knowledge in school-related activities and practice. This focus is not novel; it is coined as "funds of knowledge," from work begun nearly ten years ago. Thus, we have had the benefit of learning from those colleagues before us who have also engaged in this work. An earlier project, the Funds of Knowledge for Teaching project (González et al. 1995), for example, was based on the idea that household and community knowledge could provide significant resources for classroom practice. Central to that work was the ethnographic study of households (Moll 1992; González 1995), an approach that has been used to investigate and analyze the family history of the households of language-minority students, particularly their labor history. The experience has repeatedly revealed the accumulated bodies of knowledge and the array of skills, information, and strategies found within households, what we have referred to as funds of knowledge. Classrooms, on the other hand, are often isolated from the social world of the community, as well as its resources. Interestingly, within that world, when pertinent knowledge or resources are not readily available within the household, relationships with outside resources are activated. This contrasts sharply with what often happens within classrooms, where, for example, teachers rarely have the opportunity to access networks and draw upon resources found within the community. Additionally, while in classrooms, children may be made passive bystanders, yet within their households, they are expected to participate in a broad range of activities in the context of these social relationships. In some cases, children's participation is central to each household's functioning, as when children contribute to the economic production of the home or use their knowledge of English to facilitate the communications with outside institutions (Andrade 1998; Vásquez, Pease-Alvarez, & Shannon 1994).

What we share in Chapters Four and Five (and what is shown in other chapters in this book) are active examples of new ways in which teacher-researchers are working to bridge these and other disparities in the latest generation of this work in the Linking Home and School: A Bridge to the Many Faces of Mathematics project (BRIDGE). Unlike the earlier focus on literacy, the BRIDGE project brings the added challenge of focusing specifically on mathematical knowledge in the home and community and linking it to pedagogical innovations in the classroom, in an effort to constantly bridge the gap between students' home- and school-lived realities (see Civil 1995). In what follows we outline key components of our work, including the study group, a discussion on funds of knowledge, and the nature of our ethnographic experiences, as well as the practical applications of the same, before sharing the nature of ethnographic experiences.

How Does the Study Group Work?

Our collaboration on the project begins with the study group. The study group is both the structure and the reason for our meetings. We meet every few weeks during the school week in the late afternoon. It is the only time that teachers have to squeeze in extracurricular activities of their own choosing. Though we are all generally tired by that time, the topic of each meeting and the discussion of the group prove intellectually energizing.

The site where our meetings take place rotates from classroom to classroom, from school to school, and from district to district. Though Tucson, Arizona may not be considered a large metropolitan city, the Southwest is renowned for its geographical vastness, and this is no exception in our local travel; this project gives us an opportunity to travel to schools and communities we may not otherwise visit.

Fundamental to the study group is our establishment of relationships among the members. These relationships are fostered as we share interests and experiences. It is in this way that we begin to routinely bring forth everything else that informs our practice as teachers and researchers. It is in the study group that we are able to retell our respective experiences in the classroom and where we are able to engage one another with vivid retellings of our experiences in making a household visit (e.g., what we have seen and heard, and most important, learned, especially through the benefit of reflection). In sharing, these retellings and subsequent discussions become a part of our collective knowledge and experiences. Each consecutive study group meeting leaves us with a newfound awareness of how others experience and interpret life experiences and, in turn, challenges how we each think and feel about those same experiences. We deliberately speak of the broader experience of the study group, because there is no single event that captures it. It is a process; a holistic sense of being involved in the activity of making sense of what we see, what we come to know, and what we practice within the contexts of the classroom or the household visit.

How Do We Find Funds of Knowledge?

Building on students' strengths and on local knowledge is a commonsensical way to approach pedagogy. As was stated in Chapter One, at first blush this seems like a remarkably simple task. Yet, as shown throughout this volume, we soon encounter more complex questions that frame our work: How do we know what our students' strengths and funds of knowledge are? How do we approach the dynamic processes of the lived experiences of students without falling into assumptions about what we suppose their out-of-school experiences to be? As the BRIDGE project is geared toward *process* rather than *product,* our approach to exploring funds of knowledge has involved an ethnographic process. Rather than rely on specific techniques, we have attempted to see the familiar through an anthropological lens. Our answer to these questions focuses on the talk born of ethnography: respectful talk between people who are mutually engaged in a constructive conversation.

What Are the Methods for Ethnographic Study?

As the funds of knowledge concept has evolved in our work, and we have learned more about what works and what does not, our approach to ethnographic training has shifted. Not surprisingly, what works is exactly what our basic assumption is predicated on: the more that participants can engage and identify with the topic matter, the more interest and motivation generated. What does not work is a top-down classroom–style approach in which participants can learn methodological technique, but which strips away the multi-dimensionality of a personal ethnographic encounter. In other words, we learn ethnography by doing ethnography.

It is difficult to reduce a complex process to formulaic terms, because anything called ethnography is always in jeopardy of reductionistic misuse. However, there are certain points that are key in adopting an anthropological lens. First, it is important to read ethnographic literature. Teachers in our project have always been provided with a reader that contains numerous examples of ethnographic work relating to educational settings. Second, it is important that we develop a nonevaluative, nonjudgmental stance to the fieldwork they will be conducting. We may not always agree with what we hear, but our role is to understand how others make sense of their lives. Third, each of these activities helps us be good observers and even more, to pay attention to detail.

The household visit begins long before the actual entrance into the home. Driving down the street, we can observe the neighborhood, the surrounding area, and the external markers of what identifies this as a neighborhood. We can look for material clues to possible funds of knowledge in gardens (botanical knowledge?), patio walls (perhaps someone is a mason?), restored automobiles (mechanical knowledge?), or the nature of ornaments displayed (what is their significance? who are they made by?). During our initial exposure with ethnographic method, which takes place in the ethnographic education sessions, we show a video. This video, from an earlier project, contains two short segments of everyday community scenes. After showing the video, we ask participants to talk about what they noticed. The first video segment is that of a family yard sale and shows a great deal of activity going on at once. We stress that this is usually what happens on a household visit: life does not stand still so that we can document it in all its detail. The vignette usually elicits comments on what is being sold (wooden doll furniture might indicate carpentry skills), the interactions involved (the older siblings are caring for toddlers, indicating cross-age caretaking), and language use (code switching between Spanish and English is evident throughout). It is fascinating to notice how our own interests and our own funds of knowledge often color and filter what we observe. For example, one teacher commented that he noticed a fountain in the backyard because he was installing one himself. The second video segment is particularly rich for our BRIDGE project because it shows a nine-year-old boy in a backyard workshop, working with his father to build a barbecue grill. The scene is replete with measurement, estimation, geometry, and a range of other household mathematical practices. Because we do not often think of routine household activities as containing mathematics, this "slice of life" helps to "mathematize" the household visits.

Fourth, and perhaps most important, we ask respectful questions and learn to listen to responses. As a part of the process of entering the households, we have a series of questionnaires that explore household networks, labor histories, and daily activities. These topics have proved to be fertile areas for tapping into funds of knowledge. The questionnaires are not prescriptive and are used only as a guide to indicate the breadth and depth of possible questions. Most teachers have found that these visits begin with a question or two on family histories and continue with narratives about how families came to be where they are now. In our context, in many cases, these networks reveal strong crossborder ties with families in the northern Mexican state of Sonora, thus linking children with activities and funds of knowledge on both sides of the border. Questions on labor history have also served as one of the main sources of information on possible funds of knowledge, as skills are often embedded in work contexts. However, it is important to remember that funds of knowledge are not limited to the formal market sector. Informal market strategies, such as yard sales, selling tortillas, sewing, car repairs, and so on, can yield rich areas that can be tapped for pedagogical wealth. One outcome of respectful ethnographic talk is an increased sense of confianza, or mutual trust, as parents and teachers come to view one another in multidimensional terms.

What About Culture?

Because the term *culture* is loaded with expectations of group norms and often static ideas of how people view the world and behave in it, we have purposely avoided reference to ideas of culture. The term *culture* presumes a coherence within groups that may not exist. Instead, we have focused on *practice*, which is what households actually do and what they say about what they do. In this way, we open up a panorama of how households draw from multiple cultural systems and use these systems as strategic resources.

How Do We Make Sense of the Ethnographic Experience?

Our study groups have been key in helping us come to understand the ethnographic process. The study groups provide a safe space for BRIDGE teacher-researchers to come together and share experiences in visiting households, classroom mathematical connections, and the constraints of teaching contextualized mathematics within a prescribed curriculum. These discourses center on constructing knowledge around how children learn best and how mathematical contexts are created. In this space, we can also explore our own ideas about what we have found in the households and how it may connect to mathematical practices and further our own mathematical understanding. As we become both learners and teachers of mathematics, our insights and connection to mathematical pedagogies expand.

What Kinds of Questions Do We Ask?

It is important to remember that an interview should emerge as a type of conversation, rather than a survey or research format. We ask permission of the households first and are careful to explain that pseudonyms are always used and every effort is expended to maintain confidentiality. Based on our previous experience in household interviews, we have distilled critical topics into three basic areas. These areas correspond to three questionnaires that are generally covered in three visits. Using questionnaires as tools has been useful for teacher-ethnographers in signaling a shift in approaching the households as learners. Entering the household with questions rather than answers has provided the context for an inquiry-based visit. Questionnaires were used as guides rather than protocol, suggesting possible areas to explore and incorporating previous information as a platform for formulating new questions. Teachers have felt that the questionnaires are helpful in guiding the conversation; one teacher affirmed, "The questionnaires being used for this project represent decades of anthropological fieldwork and theory. As cultural instruments, they crystallize anthropological insight."

The first interview is based on family history and labor history. The questions are open-ended and we invite stories about families. We begin by asking how and when the family happened to be where it is now—in our case, in Tucson. This generally leads to a conversation of family roots, tracing the movements of the family from locale to locale. We also ask about other households in the region that the family may be related to or have regular contact with. This helps us conceptualize the networks within which the family operates. For example, we hear many stories of families who followed other family members to Tucson. They are then able to tap into knowledge about the area and job market that others have accumulated. The narratives that emerge from these household histories are incredibly powerful and often are testimonies to the resiliency and resources of people whose lives are often lived in the economic margins.

Teacher-researchers often come away deeply impacted by obstacles that have been overcome or by current challenges of household members. One teacher talked about an immigrant household in which fifteen people lived, with each adult member working in a labor-intensive job in order to contribute to the pool of resources. Teachers regularly encounter families whose very survival often depends on the networks of exchange that surround them. These networks are important sources for the diversity of funds of knowledge that children are exposed to. The knowledge that their grandparents, aunts and uncles, and extended family relations can tap is also a resource that goes beyond the nuclear family. We have found that the very experience of relating a family history, rich in its own complexity, often evinced a historical consciousness in parents of where they have come from and how they got to be where they are. As parents have related stories of their own mothers and fathers, grandmothers and grandfathers, life histories have come tumbling out in a fashion that was not often elucidated. Some households tell evocative stories of crossing into the United States on foot, of working in territorial mines and railroads, and of kinship networks that pulled them to their present location in Tucson. Other households tell stories of relocations and settlements, of grand matriarchs of extended families, and of their own views of community. Yet other households relay the importance of participating in local traditional ritual Easter ceremonies and the impact that these have on their children's identity. Embedded within the experience of narrating one's own particular life trajectory is the extraction of deeper meanings from our own lived experiences. As family members have narrated the stories of how they got to be where they are, everyday experiences have come to be imbued with insights and coherence that lead to alternate forms of learning. Teachers as learners, parents as learners, and students as learners can come together within learning communities in which learning is mutually educative, coconstructed, and jointly negotiated.

We have also found that labor histories are very rich sources for the funds of knowledge that households possess. However, the types of jobs and labor histories that are common within a particular location are linked to regional patterns of political economy. In our Southwestern context, we have found funds of knowledge consolidated in the ecologically pertinent arenas of mining and metallurgy, ranching and animal husbandry, ethnobotany, and transborder transactions. One interesting finding within household labor histories is that many families have approached a jack-of-all-trades strategy as a viable and necessary option in dealing with the fluctuations of the soft economy of Tucson. For non-white-collar workers, survival is often a matter of strategic shifts in employment trajectories when a particular marketable skill bottoms out. This strategy was articulated by one father, who commented, "If you want to stay in Tucson and survive, you have to be able to do everything: construction, carpentry, roofing, mechanics, or whatever. Otherwise, you'll starve." For many households who do not see relocation as an option, the economic climate of the region drives families into a wide breadth of marketable skills in a multiplicity of areas. Children are exposed not only to the funds of knowledge that these shifts engender but also to the strategic shifts in employment goals. This ability to shift strategies in midstream is a skill that the successful and productive citizen of the future must embody.

We have found family members engaged in diverse occupations that give them skills in many areas. For example, carpenters and seamstresses both engage in mathematical practices that are often intuitive, commonsensical, and not academically based. Yet these practices yield efficient and precise results, because errors are costly and can impact their livelihood. One important point to remember is that a labor history does not necessarily mean a job in the formal labor market. Many women, for example, sell items out of their homes, such as tortillas and tamales, or sell cosmetics, or have a regular stand at the local swap meet. While these are not often counted as jobs, they are ripe with potential for children's formation of knowledge. One student, for example, was able to negotiate a barter system with a fellow swap market vendor and was able to purchase particular clothes that he wanted.

The second interview is based on regular household activities. Children are often involved in ongoing household activities that can incorporate, for example, car repair, gardening, home improvement, child care, or working in a family business or hobby. One child participated in bicycle repairs and was able to acquire a high level of competency in this area. We also ask about music practices, sports, shopping with coupons, and other aspects of child life that help us develop a composite and multidimensional image of the range of possible funds of knowledge.

The third interview is the most complex, and teacher-researchers report that it is often the most revealing—and lengthy! One area of understanding processes of sense making involves how parents view and construct their roles as parents and caretakers. This interview asks questions about parenthood, about raising children, and about the experience of being a parent. Parents are asked about their own school experiences and asked to contrast them with their children's school experiences. Immigrant parents are asked about school experiences in their home country and are asked to contrast them with the educational system in the United States. There are also questions about language use for bilingual families, including when particular languages are spoken and under what circumstances.

How Is the Household Selected?

Teacher-researchers have had full flexibility to choose any child's family for a visit. Some have adopted a lottery system, picking a name at random, and others have identified particular households because they have had previous contact with them or have an interest in getting to know the families better. It is important that the families be willing to participate, are informed that they can withdraw at any time, and are aware that there is a certain time commitment involved. We are often asked if families are reluctant to be interviewed, and even though that has sometimes been the case, we have found the opposite to be true. Children often clamor to have their homes visited, and we have a standing joke that it is often easier to get into the house than it is to get out. It has been a constant source of amazement to all how often teachers have been welcomed as honored guests and with the utmost respect and courtesy. Conversations about family histories often result in the display of picture albums, yellowed newspaper clippings, and elaborate genealogies. Topics about work and hobbies often produce handcrafted items or tours of home improvement projects. Talk about schools generates diplomas and awards. Teachers are often invited back to informally participate in family gatherings or church and community functions. Telling their story becomes an important and valued experience when there is a truly engaged and interested listener and learner present.

What Happens After the Interview?

One important element in reflecting on the interview and visit resides in written field notes. We do ask for the families' permission to tape-record the interviews, since this helps in the reconstruction of the experiences. The field notes document the findings and details of a visit in a way that helps to further process the experience. The written expression of field notes helps in collectively sharing the insights gained from the visit in the study group. Following their forays into the field, teacher-researchers write up field notes, as all field workers do, based on each interview, and these field notes become the basis for the study group discussions. It is in the reflexive process involved in transcription that teachers obtain elusive insights that could otherwise be easily overlooked. For example, as they have replayed the audiotapes and referred to notes, connections and hunches have often emerged. The household begins to take on a multidimensional reality that has taken root in the interview and reached its fruition in reflexive writing. Writing gives form and substance to the connection forged between the household and the teacher. In the text that follows, Caroline Carson, coauthor of this chapter and teacher-researcher, writes about her own professional growth in the BRIDGE project as a result of the study group and subsequent household visits and classroom innovations.

My Professional Growth in the BRIDGE Project
Caroline S. Carson

I have gained a great deal of knowledge about the value in sharing and discussing the backgrounds of children and how to bring that background into the classroom to create a learning environment. Through this process I have begun to gain insights into my teaching style. The following is a rough sketch of what I have gained as an educator in the BRIDGE project, beginning especially during the second year, as my experiences and reflections have begun to fall into place. The BRIDGE project has been instrumental in helping me to reflect on my teaching style from many different viewpoints. Through research articles, interviews, formal and informal discussions, and classroom videos, I have been able to reflect on my educational growth.

At the beginning of my second year in the program I was unsure of my direction, based solely on the previous year's work. I knew that I would be implementing more "home-based" knowledge into my curriculum. By "home-based" knowledge, I mean information I had acquired from my home visits. At our retreat the year prior, I had worked on a math curriculum unit with cooking as the theme. I was now thinking that I would be using cooking to teach an area in mathematics after I completed my interviews for this year.

Aside from these curriculum ideas, I began to realize that there were a lot of ways I could continue to grow in my teaching profession. For example, I realized that the way I conducted math classes was primarily teacher-student-directed, with small-group discussion. I wanted to grow as a professional! It was not enough to make the curriculum engaging, I wanted to reflect on my teaching experiences and practice, in order to grow as a teacher.

After several formal meetings with the members of the BRIDGE study group, I began to feel that I wanted more documentation and evaluation of how I was teaching mathematics in my fifth-grade classroom. I knew that evaluating how I was teaching would help me to incorporate the students' home-based knowledge into our mathematics curriculum. I wanted to work on curriculum, too, but I felt I needed to see what was already going on in my classroom.

This form of evaluation stemmed from an article we had read in the study group on classroom language, "When the Problem Is Not the Question and the Solution Is Not the Answer: Mathematical Knowing and Teaching," by Magdalene Lampert (1990). This article opened up my eyes to the importance of teacher and student discourse in the classroom. I realized that it is through appropriate discourse that a process of coming to know and understand math can take place. Unlike before, I no longer believed that the correct answer to a problem was the same as a student knowing the reason for that correct answer. This was a turning point for me. In her article, Lampert states, "Research in educational anthropology suggests that the teacher can initiate patterns to build a participation structure that redefines the roles and responsibilities of both teacher and students in relation to learning and knowing" (34). This research sparked my interest further, because in my own classroom I also wanted to promote a discourse among all of us, a discourse that would encourage the problem-solving process.

Lampert illustrates how the use of language can be instrumental in assisting discourse. She presented students with mathematical vocabulary that helped them with their discussions. At one of our BRIDGE study group meetings, it was pointed out that to use a specific vocabulary might hinder or not take into account the students' own vocabulary. It was a lively discussion that really prodded me into talking about ideas regarding the use of language in the classroom. I was coming closer to what I wanted to try to do in the classroom the following year, in terms of language and student discourse.

This process of discovery (which is both personal and professional) is symbolic of the BRIDGE project and the benefits that are reaped by participating in it. The project has this year afforded me the opportunity to grow as an educator. I was able to discuss my goal and personal desire for self-growth with other teachers, which helped to structure the way to begin this process (though it had already begun through the reflection). The project also provided the necessary video equipment and materials to videotape some of my math classes. I was, for the first time, able to see firsthand what I was doing during the math lesson! As follow-up, several BRIDGE staff members helped me to focus on looking at the videos based on Lampert's "Language Indicators." Additionally, other project members began to look at some of these same videos with CREDE's "Standards for Effective Pedagogy," in order to identify and compare effective teaching strategies. While the videos can be approached in a number of ways, having approached them with a particular focus was useful. As a result, I was able to concentrate on language and discourse in depth, then apply what I had learned to the classroom. As an example, I am continually taking back ideas to the study group for support and to generate even more discussion with questions such as How do I shift from a teacher-directed classroom to a student-directed classroom? or How can I incorporate language into the instruction to encourage dialogue amongst the students that is appropriate to their own language use?

These questions are reflective of what this program has been for me. It is about the process of growth in learning from a community at large and a community of professionals that share their knowledge. In a sense, the BRIDGE study group is a role model for how to grow educationally in a group, which is what I want my own students to do in the classroom. As professionals in the study group, we have established the practice of sharing from our knowledge and experience base—which can offer new insights for someone else in the group or help us understand further.

In a sense, my philosophy of teaching is dynamic and BRIDGE is aiding me in keeping the teaching and learning of mathematics alive and meaningful. At one time, I thought that we were replicating curricula that were already in existence, but the more I reflect on this, I realize that I am growing as a professional in this project. Equally important, I am also able to share this growth with other interested professionals. Additionally, I am learning how to gather data from research to present it to others. I hope to eventually be able to present my work to a large body of educators, as I have already begun to do at the 1999 meeting of the National Council on the Teaching of Mathematics in San Francisco. This is another challenge, but one I embrace as I continue the process of learning to teach from my students and other professionals.

What Are the Implications of These Study Groups?

It would be all too easy to answer some of the questions raised within the study group sessions by quickly dismissing what some do as mathematics by validating formal application over informal practices. But, we have the burden to understand the social and cultural practices in which mathematics is embedded. We do, however, agree that mathematics is a gatekeeper. In doing so, we have begun to realize the ways in which we often measure others' knowledge of mathematics with the yardstick of testing, which values certain knowledge and experiences as superior, while qualifying as inferior (via remuneration and prestige, for example) other less palpable expressions of mathematical knowledge. We are also finding that some of these perceptions are closely related to gender- and class-specific knowledge and experiences of individuals; this is an area that we are just now beginning to explore. That mathematics is not a gender or culturally or socially neutral subject should be of no surprise, but we are usually taught that it is not (see Walkerdine 1988). This is again an area that we will continue exploring as we pursue the activities of the study group. The significance of the study group notwithstanding, it is first a forum for the process of consciousness about pedagogy, curriculum, and knowledge in the teaching and learning of mathematics. It is also a vehicle for forging the links between home and school knowledge and experience in the creation of innovative curriculum and pedagogy in mathematics.

What Are the Implications of the Household Studies?

Despite our better sense to do otherwise, somewhere, sometime during our formal preparation in education, myths and stereotypes about parents and especially minority, language-minority, and working-class families are woven in and reinforced time and time again (Flores, Tefft Cousin, & Díaz 1991). This is not an exception even within our study group. However, the very nature of the ethnographic experience and later analysis of the data collected, coupled with the ongoing teacher-researcher study groups, challenges and transforms those counterproductive and misguided perceptions that have served to limit the ebb and flow of knowledge and experiences between home and classroom.

One particular series of household visits by teacher-researcher Caroline Carson makes the case for the importance of the ethnographic experiences of the project. During the second year of the project, Caroline chose to switch the focus of her household visits to single-parent homes, given their growing numbers within her classroom and school. She visited one particular family headed by a single mother with four children. Initially, the visit was typical in that it was informative and enjoyable; the student was proud to have his teacher visit his home. During the course of the visit, Caroline learned much about the routine that the family had, duties and responsibilities of the children, and so on. She also began to learn about the family's labor and educational history. However, this and subsequent visits eventually revealed that the family had been homeless, living in a car and moving from shelter to shelter for a period following the father's profound substance abuse and later during his subsequent separation from the family. Eventually the parents divorced. However, from the early history of the family, Caroline culled out important details. For example, she found that the father and mother, children of Mexican immigrants, had been raised in the Midwest in homes where the education and work ethic were important, as it has been in all homes we have visited. Both parents graduated high school and had some postsecondary education. The father had a number of experiences (e.g., construction) that reinforced his own mathematical knowledge and abilities, as was evidenced in the

way he taught the older children mathematics, while the mother taught other subjects during an earlier period of more stable family life in which they were homeschooling the children.

While there are many more details shared by Caroline about her visits, the point of this brief vignette is that despite the numerous factors for being at risk (poverty, homelessness, divorce, minority status, etc.), this family challenged any labeling. That this family history was not known to the school may have been significant in averting any labeling. At present the children are doing well academically, with the exception of the youngest one, a second grader, who among other things did not have the benefit of both parents' homeschooling but was caught in that awkward period of transition. The older daughters are enrolled in alternative academies and also doing well and helping at home.

During a study group meeting, Caroline expressed the impression this family had left on her; she shared that though materially speaking, they were not wealthy, there was a wealth of love, respect, and discipline. This, suggested Caroline, was a family for us all to learn from; it had also taught her a great deal about respecting families and about a family's own resilience during difficult periods. This is the essence of the very nature of experiences that are shared by teacher-researchers following household visits; other household knowledge and experiences begin to build on this foundation.

We have learned that before we can begin discussing the academic potential for household knowledge, it is necessary to cull out, as Caroline did, the social and historical contexts of each family in order to appreciate the struggles it faces. At the same time, in sharing the stories of a family, as in Caroline's case, it is inevitable that one will bring one's own experiences and knowledge to the table; in this way, teachers themselves are exploring their own funds of knowledge.

References

Andrade, R. 1998. "Life in Elementary School: Children's Ethnographic Reflections." In *Students as Researchers of Culture and Language in Their Own Communities*, ed. A. Egan-Robertson & D. Bloome, 93–114. Cresskill, NJ: Hampton Press.

Civil, M. 1995. Everyday Mathematics, "Mathematicians' Mathematics," and School Mathematics: Can We (Should We) Bring These Three Cultures Together? Paper presented at the annual meeting of the American Educational Research Association, San Francisco, CA, April.

Flores, B., P. Tefft Cousin, & E. Díaz. 1991. "Transforming Deficit Myths About Learning, Language, and Culture." *Language Arts* 68: 369–79.

González, N. 1995. "Processual Approaches to Multicultural Education." *Journal of Applied Behavioral Science* 31 (2): 234–44.

González, N., L. Moll, M. Floyd Tenery, A. Rivera, P. Rendón, R. Gonzáles, & C. Amanti. 1995. "Funds of Knowledge for Teaching in Latino Households." *Urban Education* 29 (4): 443–71.

Lampert, M. 1990. "When the Problem Is Not the Question and the Solution Is Not the Answer: Mathematical Knowing and Teaching." *American Educational Research Journal* 27 (1): 29–63.

Moll, L. C. 1992. "Bilingual Classroom Studies and Community Analysis." *Educational Researcher* 21 (2): 20–24.

National Council of Teachers of Mathematics, Commission on Standards for School Mathematics. 1989. *Curriculum and Evaluation Standards for School Mathematics.* Reston, VA.

Vásquez, O., L. Pease-Alvarez, & S. M. Shannon. 1994. *Pushing Boundaries: Language and Culture in a Mexicano Community.* Cambridge, MA: Cambridge University Press.

Walkerdine, V. 1988. *The Mastery of Reason: Cognitive Development and the Production of Rationality.* New York: Routledge.

11

Seeing, Believing, and Taking Action

NORMA GONZÁLEZ, ELLEN MCINTYRE
& ANN ROSEBERY

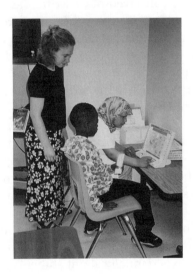

Many people have remarked on the challenges confronting teachers who face children each morning from lives far from their own, especially now when that challenge can determine teachers' success across the country. For many years I thought the problem could be alleviated, even if not solved, by providing information about cultural differences as a part of pre-service and in-service education. . . . Instead, a more helpful process seems to be for teachers to learn experientially about students and families, and in the process to reflect on their own personal and cultural background instead of unthinkingly living it as

an unexamined norm. But saying that only changes the terms of the problem; solving it is now up to each teacher.

— COURTNEY CAZDEN 1999, VII–VIII

This is a book by and for teachers. It is an effort to share stories about the ways that some teachers are addressing the issues involved in teaching children "from lives far from their own," to use Cazden's words. Its audience is teachers who want to go beyond their classrooms and their training, who want to push the boundaries of effective practices to solve the dynamic and ever-changing puzzle that is learning and teaching.

This book was not conceived of or written as a one-size-fits-all pedagogical prescription. Indeed, many of the stories may be context-specific. We do not claim that teaching practices that are effective in Appalachia will play out equally well in New York or New Mexico. Even within the same school district, particular programs, projects, and practices may not transfer well. But that is precisely the strength and promise of the kinds of ethnographic approaches to teaching described in this book. Because they are rooted in specific locales and particular local histories, they can help teachers observe, hear, and learn about the particulars of students, families, and communities. To be successful, teachers must ultimately engage with the complexity of educating their particular children. They must have data to guide pedagogical decisions about which aspects of best practices are most suited to their children.

Does this point of view problematize matters for teachers? Absolutely. As Cazden's quote at the beginning of this chapter suggests, it is now up to each teacher to "learn experientially about students and families, and in the process to reflect on [her or his] own personal and cultural background." One of the premises of this book is that neither children, their households, nor their communities are static; social processes are ever in motion. Thus, no single characterization can capture the breadth and depth of any community. However, as these stories show, teachers can study and subsequently marshal local knowledge as a platform for teaching and learning.

These stories can help conceptualize tools for action when designing rigorous and challenging curricula intended to capitalize on a foundation of locally constructed knowledge. The stories in this book describe how teachers have tapped into a wide range of information—parent knowledge, student knowledge, community knowledge, and their own knowledge—in an attempt to create such curricula.

Knowing the Children

All good teachers think deeply about the children they teach. The teachers in this book share a simple premise and have explored its implications for their children's learning: children learn best when abstract principles are conveyed to them in terms that reflect their own knowledge base. This does not mean that teachers teach only what children or their households already know, but that the students' funds of knowledge are the basis for curricular and pedagogical ends. Knowing the children and their families is one way to begin this learning cycle. Ayers (1993) tells us,

> Teaching is an interactive practice that begins and ends with seeing the student. This is more complicated than it seems, for it is something that is ongoing and never completely finished. The student grows and changes, the teacher learns, the situation shifts, and seeing becomes an evolving challenge. As layers of mystification and obfuscation are peeled away, as the student becomes more fully present to the teacher, experience and ways of thinking and knowing that were initially obscure become ground on which real teaching can be constructed. (25)

There are examples of this kind of seeing in several chapters. Sharon Maher in Chapter Two struggled to find ways of seeing her students and their families on the Zuni Pueblo. Her challenge was made more difficult by the community's reluctance to allow outsiders to participate in many aspects of Zuni life. Sharon insightfully realized, however, that her students could be her informants. By designing her lessons so that students analyzed the activities, values, and traditions of two communities—their own and the fictitious community in *Fiddler on the Roof*—she helped her students learn how to write compare and contrast texts and she learned about the local Zuni community. In a similar way, Pilar Coto and her colleagues in Chapter Six listened purposively to their preschoolers' questions and enlisted the help of parents in doing the same in an effort to get to know the children. This gave them a child-centered foundation for making decisions about what to do next in their study of chicks and, in a very real sense, helped them shape their curriculum to the children's interests and experiences. JoAnn Archie in Chapter Eight, who lives in the community in which she teaches, makes efforts to pay attention to families' voices and activities in the neighborhood. She meets the parents of her students at church, the grocery store, and favorite community restaurants. She knows where her students live and who their neighbors are. She plans her curricular studies, such as her history unit, with the perspectives and experiences of her students in mind. Likewise, Vivette Blackwell in

Chapter Three comes from the community in which she teaches, and thus builds on the rhetorical and linguistic patterns that are familiar to her students. Effective teachers make an ongoing effort to understand their students' home and school lives at deep and contextualized levels, and they organize instruction in ways that enhance and build on what students do know.

Getting Past a Deficit View of Children

How teachers see their students directly influences how they treat them, what they expect of them, and subsequently what students learn. When children are viewed as less-formed adults, as persons with deficient language, as lacking skills they "should" have, or as "culturally deprived," they learn less. The teachers in this book never viewed their children as deficient. In fact, they saw children's experiences as gifts to be shared with others, strengths on which to build curricula, and opportunities for celebration. These are teachers who are not afraid to cocreate curricula, even on topics they know little about. Again quoting Ayers, there are many questions that can guide teachers as they attempt to learn about their students:

> Who is this person before me? What are his interests and areas of wonder? How does she express herself and what is her awareness of herself as a learner? What effort and potential does she bring? (1993, 29)

As teachers seek answers to these questions, they will find that parents are crucial, and underutilized, sources of information. Unfortunately, parents may also be discounted as key sources of information because they are viewed through the same "deficit" lens that is turned on their children. Yet, because parents have spent so much time with their children, they are bound to have deep understandings of their growth and development. Here is how Stacy Greer, one of the teachers in Chapter Seven who helped create the Agricultural Field Day at Cane Creek Elementary School, views what she can learn from parents:

> The parents have so much information that I would never have known— what the child likes, hobbies, how the child deals with stress. They've spent six years with the child, or seven, or eight. And they have that much expertise which I am trying to catch up.

For Stacy and her colleague Ruth Ann, parents play a crucial role in creating a successful learning environment.

In Chapter Four, when Leslie Kahn decided on her garden curriculum for her elementary classroom after visiting the homes of students who had gardens, she enlisted the support of parents through collecting books on

Navajo rugs and weaving, inviting them to volunteer in the garden, asking them to donate seed, soil, and flats of pansies and tomatoes, and asking some to demonstrate the use of a loom. One grandmother talked to the class about weavings in Latin America. Vivette Blackwell in Chapter Three also used parents as resources for community-oriented lessons, and for those who could not get to the school, she designed "family" homework that would excite and engage all members of the family.

The teachers in this book all share the view that parents and community are integral to their children's education; they involve them in the classroom instructional program in a variety of ways throughout the year.

Becoming Learners

It is clear that the teachers portrayed in this book made conscious efforts to learn about the backgrounds of their students. But what may be less clear is that they are students of the disciplines they teach as well as of innovative pedagogies. The instruction depicted in these chapters is not "funsy-wunsy" (Cambourne 1988), nor watered down to make children happy. It is high-level academic work that engages students as intelligent, capable learners. These instructional programs are the direct result of ongoing learning on the part of teachers.

Caroline Carson's story of her own learning in Chapter Ten is one compelling example of how a teacher learns both about her students and her discipline in order to be the teacher she needs to be for her students. Through the BRIDGE project study groups, Caroline visited families in an effort to seek out and understand funds of knowledge; read and discussed articles on pedagogy and mathematics; analyzed herself and others on videotape; talked with other teachers; and constantly questioned her own work. She has learned that teaching is not a static activity, but an ever-evolving one that must be continually refined as the field grows and both we and our students change.

Josiane Hudicourt-Barnes' students in Chapter Five had trouble understanding what she assumed would be a routine science lesson on pitch and volume. Their nonacceptance of her view of these concepts led her to literally review pitch and volume, to take another look at what had heretofore been unexamined for her. In this way, she came to see that these concepts were far less black and white than she'd thought; her understanding of pitch and volume were enhanced as she struggled to engage her students with them.

In Vivette Blackwell's classroom, described in Chapter Three, the teacher learns along with her students. The expectation is that the classroom is a learning environment and that learning will happen there. Vivette uses adult vocabulary with her third graders, not watered-down language some think is appropriate for primary grade students. The class literally celebrates when students learn beyond expectations. In fact, the expectation is that *all* children will learn at high levels and the children know this. Vivette, too, expects herself to learn along with her students. All the teachers in this book ask themselves what they can learn from their students as well as what they can teach them.

Forming Communities of Learners

We are all experienced in the life of a community—indeed, many communities. Communities of practice, as Wenger (1998) points out, pervade our everyday lives at home, at work, at school, at church, and in our extracurricular activities. They are the informal assemblages of people, relationships, practices, artifacts, symbols, conventions, stories, and histories to which we belong and give shape. It is important to distinguish them from the formal institutions in which they often reside. The various chapters in this book in one way or another are concerned with the creation of communities of learning. A learning community is characterized by deep connections between everyday and schooled knowledge and practices and the ways those connections are explored as the foundation for enhancing learning and teaching.

The learning communities described in this book take many forms and involve a variety of members: teachers, students, parents, farmers, barbers, drummers, scientists, and mathematicians. Traditional relationships—such as those between teacher and student, scientist and teacher, parent and child, and teacher and parent—are being changed and formed anew in these communities. Questions are being explored about the relationship between everyday and schooled knowledge and practices in disciplines such as science, mathematics, history, and literature; about the relation of home, community, disciplinary, and cultural practices to learning; and about the meaning of such constructs as context and discourse. For example, in Chapter Nine, José David Fonseca describes how he was able to perceive the dispersed knowledge in the community in the area of construction and building as a platform for motivating students and as a base for sophisticated mathematical functions. Drawing from the learned community, he solicited information from real estate companies; he also drew from his own knowledge of drafting, architecture, and engineering.

The formation of a learning community is never simple nor straightforward. It is necessary to move beyond a straightforward and unilineal bridging of household knowledge and school knowledge. Rather, it involves an acknowledgment that all knowledge has elements of the abstract and the concrete, theory and practice, the particular and the universal. Forming learning communities then becomes an exercise in drawing from these multiple knowledge bases in a way that is accessible to students.

Basing Instruction in Context

As we indicated in the acknowledgments, the work described in this volume is part of a larger program of research on teaching and learning conducted at the Center for Research on Education, Diversity, and Excellence (CREDE). The stories in this book bring to life one of the basic principles that has emerged from CREDE's research program: teaching, curriculum, and school itself should be contextualized within the experiences, and skills of local communities. Those involved in this research share a theoretical perspective concerning the social nature of learning, assuming that learning is socially mediated (Vygotsky 1978). Each of the chapters has illustrated how aspects of context can support and enhance the learning process.

One underlying premise of these perspectives is that instruction always takes place within a context. The question then becomes whether the context is meaningful to the students, relevant to the resources they bring with them to the classroom, and able to support development of perspectives from within a discipline such as mathematics, history, science, or literature. Instruction in context, then, has multiple levels. At one level, the idea of context has to do with trying to connect learning in a discipline with children's learning in their everyday experiences, that is, their lives out of school. The key transformation then becomes the exploration of how to ground their learning of mathematics and science, for example, in everyday experience, while at the same time helping them acquire academic mathematics or science.

At a second level, instruction in context incorporates curricular practices that address literacy, numeracy, and science practices mediated through community-based experiences that afford students opportunities to apply skills acquired in both home and school contexts. A third level of context includes educators and the school, as the learning environment itself is contextualized as a social process. This includes the participation of teachers as researchers of their children's learning and their classroom practices as well as incorporation of parents as resources within the learning process and the validation of local and community funds of knowledge.

The approach that views the school as nestled in the community provides broader contexts that affect students and classroom practices. Not only is context in this broad conceptualization a theoretical construct, but it is situated within the real and lived experiences of students and their families. At a larger level, the very real economic impact of marginalization on students is a context that we cannot gloss over. An example from the BRIDGE project makes this clear: a teacher asked students how they use mathematics in the home, and one child, when relating items that can be counted, piped up that she counts the number of pots on the floor when it is raining and the roof leaks.

The innovations described in this book are the result of integrating teacher learning, teaching practices, and student learning. They highlight the strong commitment of those involved to developing and understanding the underlying connections among teacher professional development, pedagogical reform, student learning, and achievement in academic subject areas. It is important to note that although the teachers depicted in this volume have come to see the "terms of the problem," as Cazden says, in similar ways, none of them is trying to solve the problem on his or her own. At the same time that they are creating contextualized instruction for their students, they are active members of teaching and learning communities that are nurturing their own professional growth. These communities are made up of fellow teachers and researchers, and sometimes parents and community members join them. These communities become places where teachers can ask questions about themselves and their children, probe their understandings of the disciplines they teach, and examine long-held assumptions about what is good for whom and when in the classroom. At their best, such learning communities are powerful forums for teacher professional development, which, in turn, enable teachers to create classroom communities of learning that are responsive to all children.

References

Ayers, W. 1993. *To Teach: The Journey of a Teacher.* New York: Teachers College Press.

Cambourne, B. 1988. *The Whole Story: Natural Learning and the Acquisition of Literacy in the Classrooom.* Portsmouth, NH: Heinemann.

Cazden, C. 1999. Foreword to *Teaching Other People's Children: Literacy and Learning in a Bilingual Classroom,* by C. Ballenger. New York: Teachers College Press.

Vygotsky, L. S. 1978. *Mind in Society: The Development of Higher Psychological Processes.* Cambridge, MA: Harvard University Press.

Wenger, E. 1998. *Communities of Practice: Learning, Meaning and Identity.* Cambridge: Cambridge University Press.

Contributors

Editors

Ellen McIntyre is an associate professor of education at the University of Louisville, Kentucky where she teaches graduate courses in literacy research and theory and studies young children's literacy development in and out of school contexts.

Ann Rosebery is codirector of the Cheche Konnen Center at TERC in Cambridge, Massachusetts, which is dedicated to improving science education for poor and minority students.

Norma González is an associate research anthropologist in the Bureau of Applied Research in Anthropology at the University of Arizona who specializes in anthropology and education.

Other Contributors (in Alphabetical Order)

Jim Allen has been a preschool teacher since 1982 and is currently teaching at the Neighborhood Child Care Center in Santa Cruz, California. He enjoys doing theatre with young children.

Rosi Andrade is a research associate at the Southwest Institute for Research on Women in the Department of Women's Studies, University of Arizona. Her interests are the social, cultural, and political experiences of minority children and their parents, especially mothers, and capitalizing on expanding the nature and types of reading and mathematics experiences of children as a means to personal development and empowerment.

JoAnn Archie is an elementary teacher and primary reading consultant in an urban school in the Jefferson County School District in Louisville, Kentucky.

Melanie Ayers is a graduate from the Department of Education at the University of Arizona, where she received her master's degree in teaching and teacher education. She works as a software trainer at Rincon Research Corporation in Tucson, Arizona.

Maureen Callanan is a professor of psychology at the University of California–Santa Cruz, where she teaches courses in developmental psychology. Her research focuses on early cognitive and language development in the context of family conversations.

Caroline Carson has a M.A. in elementary education from the Bank Street College. She has taught in New York City public schools, a Quaker school in Costa Rica, and public school (grades 4–6) in Tucson, Arizona. She is currently enjoying being the mother of two sons.

Marta Civil is an associate professor of mathematics education at the University of Arizona, where she teaches mathematics courses for preservice and practicing teachers. Her research interests are in the areas of connecting in-school and out-of-school mathematics and of parental involvement in mathematics.

Faith R. Conant has a master's degree in ethnomusicology and has conducted ethnographic work on traditional drumming in Togo, West Africa, under a Fulbright research grant, and on science learning in Haitan Creole-speaking classroom communities in Cambridge, Massachusetts, for the Cheche Konnen project at TERC.

Pilar Coto teaches preschoolers in Spanish and English at the Neighborhood Child Care Center in Santa Cruz, California. Her main interest is bilingual education and she enjoys learning from students.

Cherie Crandall, formerly a lawyer, has been a director of various preschools for the past fifteen years. Her expertise is in the areas of program development and of creating a caring community for families and staff.

Georgia Epaloose is a curriculum and professional development specialist for the Zuni public schools in Zuni, New Mexico. She coordinates the district-developed curriculum and provides professional development in the area of effective teaching strategies for Native American students.

José David Fonseca has taught middle and high school mathematics in Tucson, Arizona. He is currently enrolled in a doctoral program at the University of Arizona.

Michele L. Foster is a professor in the Center for Educational Studies at Claremont Graduate University, where she teaches courses and conducts research broadly focused on the social, cultural, and sociolinguistic contexts of learning for African Americans.

Stacy Greer has been a primary teacher in a rural school in Kentucky, for ten years.

Josiane Hudicourt-Barnes is currently a researcher and professional development specialist at TERC. She has been a teacher and administrator in Haitian bilingual programs in both Cambridge and Boston, Massachusetts.

Leslie H. Kahn is an intermediate multiage classroom teacher who enjoys working with her students and discovering new ways of teaching mathematics.

Sharon Maher is a middle school language arts teacher at the Zuni Middle School in Zuni, New Mexico. Her classroom emphasizes effective teaching strategies for Native American students and Glasser's quality instruction.

Ligia Miranda, orginally from Costa Rica, had more than ten years' experience as a bilingual resource teacher in elementary schools before she moved into a preschool setting. She was a teacher at the Neighborhood Child Care Center in Santa Cruz, California, when Chapter Six was written.

Colleen Murphy received her B.A. in child development in 1988. She taught preschool for nearly ten years, specializing in staff training and the creative arts. Currently she is a full-time mother for son Skyler.

Tryphenia B. Peele is a doctoral candidate in the School of Educational Studies at Claremont Graduate University. A former elementary teacher, Peele received the 1995 AERA Spencer Research Fellowship. Her research interests include sociocultural studies, qualitative and ethnographic research methods, and issues related to the education of African American children.

Anne Striffler worked at various preschools in the Monterey Bay area for nine years. In 1998 she moved into parent education and is now director/teacher of the Watsonville Parent Co-Op Preschool for Watsonville/Aptos adult education.

Ruth Ann Sweazy has been a primary teacher for six years in a rural school in Kentucky.

Roland Tharp is the director of the Center for Research on Education, Diversity, and Excellence (CREDE) and a professor of education and psychology at the University of California–Santa Cruz. In 1993 he received (with Ronald Gallimore) the prestigious Grawemeyer Award in education for the book *Rousing Minds to Life: Teaching, Learning, and Schooling in Social Context.*

Beth Warren is codirector of the Cheche Konnen Center at TERC in Cambridge, Massachusetts, where she conducts research on children's sense making in science and teaching as a practice of discipline-based inquiry.

Index